Power, Politics, and Adult Educational Administration

This book seeks to draw out the impacts of power, politics, and critical theory on the growth of adult learning in a small liberal arts college setting. Using critical theory as an analytical tool to investigate questions around budgeting, academic quality, and student access, this volume shows how these issues are inextricably bound up with those of hegemony, ideology, and bureaucratic rationality. The author demonstrates, too, how acknowledging these influences at the outset leads to a sustainable and equitable adult learning environment. Through an emphasis on both organizational context and individual learning experiences, this volume contributes new substance to the understanding of politics and power relationships in educational leadership.

John Kokolus is the Founding Dean of the School of Continuing and Professional Studies at Elizabethtown College, USA.

Power, Politics, and Adult Educational Administration
The Case of a Liberal Arts Institution

John Kokolus

NEW YORK AND LONDON

First published 2019
by Routledge
711 Third Avenue, New York, NY 10017

and by Routledge
2 Park Square, Milton Park, Abingdon, Oxon, OX14 4RN

Routledge is an imprint of the Taylor & Francis Group, an informa business

© 2019 Taylor & Francis

The right of John Kokolus to be identified as author of this work has been asserted by him in accordance with sections 77 and 78 of the Copyright, Designs and Patents Act 1988.

All rights reserved. No part of this book may be reprinted or reproduced or utilized in any form or by any electronic, mechanical, or other means, now known or hereafter invented, including photocopying and recording, or in any information storage or retrieval system, without permission in writing from the publishers.

Trademark notice: Product or corporate names may be trademarks or registered trademarks, and are used only for identification and explanation without intent to infringe.

Library of Congress Cataloguing in Publication Data
A catalog record for this title has been requested.

ISBN: 978-0-367-15194-2 (hbk)
ISBN: 978-0-429-05565-2 (ebk)

Typeset in Times New Roman
by Deanta Global Publishing Services, Chennai, India

Contents

1 Introduction 1

2 Continuing Education Timeline at Elizabethtown
College: 1899–2014 15

PART ONE
Beginnings 27

3 Partnerships in Adult Education and the Impact of
Critical Theory 29

4 Critical Theory's Structural Democratic Impulse 32

5 Challenges to the Status Quo 35

PART TWO
Accreditation and the Continuing Education Plan 37

6 Self-Studies: 1998 and 2009 39

7 New Plan for Continuing Education – Part I 43

PART THREE
Faculty 49

8 New Plan for Continuing Education – Part II 51

9 New Plan for Continuing Education – Part III 55

PART FOUR
Locations 61

10 New Plan for Continuing Education – Part IV 63

PART FIVE
Class Conflict 67

11 Conflicts between Adult and Traditional Students 69

PART SIX
Staff 73

12 Stresses and Strains of Critical Theory on the Front Line 75

PART SEVEN
The Rhetoric of Academic Quality 79

13 Faculty Assessment Process as a Gateway for
    Affiliated Faculty 81

Conclusion 85
References 97
Index 98

1 Introduction

Between 2000 and 2015, Elizabethtown College (EC), a small, non-profit, liberal arts institution of higher education (IHE), developed a robust adult learner degree-completion program that ran parallel to its traditional residential student program; this traditional program was stabilized around 1,800 full-time, residential students. Located in rural south-central Pennsylvania, equidistant between Lancaster, York, and Harrisburg, EC was an unlikely candidate for success with adult learners, offering associates, bachelors, and masters degrees. But over the course of 15 years, the number of adult learners grew from less than 98 to more than 800, the vast majority of whom were part-time; and graduate programs (a little over 100 graduate students) were added to a healthy number of undergraduate programs. Undergraduate majors included: accounting, business administration, human services, human services-behavioral counseling, criminal justice, corporate communications, health care administration, and information systems. Business administration, criminal justice, health care administration, human services, and human services-behavioral counseling were also available online as well as on campus. Graduate programs included: the MBA (available online or blended or on campus) and the MSL, Master of Strategic Leadership (available blended or on campus). The number of locations where programs were offered tripled from two to six, thereby "saturating" the potential regional market. Gross revenues from adult programming grew from approximately $500,000 per annum to approximately $7,000,000 per annum, the latter figure comprising 8% to 10% of EC's total revenues. Annual net revenue grew from $5,000 to approximately $4,000,000 and online delivery of courses grew to 67% of total courses offered.

What happened at this small, independent, liberal arts college affiliated with the Church of the Brethren that made such growth possible? How did power, politics, and critical theory configure themselves to encourage the growth of adult learning? How did they configure themselves to suppress it? Why are these questions important? What do their answers tell us about adult learning? What do they tell us about higher education in general?

2 Introduction

Change is sometimes simple; in this case it was not. A multiplicity of actors, motivations, structures, and visions vied for attention and resources. Valuing analysis more highly than narrative or description, I have borrowed two tools to impose a simple analytic order upon events at EC from 2000 to 2015. The first tool comes from the analytical framework developed by Bolman and Deal (2013) .This provides sets of perspectives called frames, through which to approach and view the events of the decade and a half under consideration – perspectives that lend coherence to the jumble of events that took place over this time period. The second tool is critical theory as understood and as articulated by Brookfield (2005), which I have used to analyze important events at a deeper level than Bolman and Deal's (2013) larger framework allows.

Relying on these two analytical tools, I analyze selected topics about what happened and why during the decade and a half of change in adult learning at EC. I ask the reader to keep in mind that I have interpreted and applied these tools liberally, knowing that they might be applied differently than the way I have chosen to apply them. The resulting analysis helps to clarify the roles and relationships of power, politics, critical theory, and the growth of adult learning. From this clarification, I draw some conclusions, lessons, and recommendations from what went on during this decade and a half. I emphasize that these conclusions, lessons, and recommendations are not the only ones that can be reasonably drawn based on this chosen analysis, just the most compelling ones in my judgment.

Bolman and Deal's (2013) very useful analytical framework based on different frames of reference through which to understand and guide organizational behavior is a major contribution to our understanding of how organizations develop and behave. The four frames helped me organize and analyze events at EC when the college developed a robust adult learner degree completion program from 2000 to 2015. Taken together, these frames constitute a holistic, broadly interpretive framework which includes:

- The Structural Frame (Basic and Dense)
  - Organizations exist to accomplish established goals.
  - For any organization, an appropriate structure can be designed and implemented.
  - Structure ensures that people focus on getting the specific job done.
  - Structural specialization permits higher levels of individual expertise and performance.
  - Coordination, control, and their appropriate configuration are essential to effectiveness.
  - Organizational problems originate from inappropriate structures and/or their configuration and can be resolved through reorganization, restructuring, and/or reconfiguration.

- The Human Resource Frame (Human Needs)
  - Organizations exist to serve human needs. (Can easily be lost as human resource instruments institutionalize.)
  - Organizations and people need each other.
  - When the fit between the individual and the organization is poor, one or both will suffer.
  - When the fit between the individual and the organization is good, both benefit.
- The Political Frame (Priorities and Allocation of Resources)
  - Important decisions involve allocation of scarce resources. (These decision makers may be decentralized or centralized; they may operate openly or operate in a more hidden fashion.)
  - Organizations are composed of coalitions and interest groups who vie with each other for scarce resources.
  - Goals and decisions emerge from bargaining, negotiating, and jockeying for power that can leave residues of bad feelings.
  - Power and conflict are central features of organizational life.
  - Power and conflict among stakeholders may remain hidden behind facades that cover them.
- The Symbolic Frame (Organization Members Impart Meaning to Organizational Characteristics and Behavior)
  - What matters in an organization is not what happens but what it means to participants; this can cover a diversity of meanings.
  - Faced with uncertainty and ambiguity, people create symbols to resolve confusion, increase predictability, and provide direction; people seek stability and psychological certainty.
  - Organizations have distinct cultures that may be positive or negative, strong or weak.
  - Myths, rituals, and ceremonies help people find meaning in their organizational experience (Bolman & Deal, 2013).

My analysis relies on the fluidity and flexibility of inter-frame boundaries; I try to avoid rigidity in these boundaries and I try to encourage the flow of knowledge and intellectual goods between frames.

Each of the four frames generates its own unique leadership style. Thus:

- Structural Leadership (Associated with Gross Structures)
  - Clarifies organizational goals.
  - Develops clear rules and effective procedures.
  - Defines roles and clarifies responsibilities.
  - Clarity of structure and function are valued by these leaders.

- Human Resource Leadership (Associated with Human Need)
  - Identifies peoples' needs.
  - Offers personal support.
  - Recognizes participants' strengths.
  - Provides opportunities for growth.
  - Encourages the transformation of general human nature into specific human personality.
- Political Leadership (Associated with Priorities and Allocation of Resources)
  - Understands distribution of resources.
  - Identifies major constituencies.
  - Builds coalitions.
  - Assesses risks and opportunities.
  - Negotiates differences and reaches compromises.
  - Values conflict resolution skills.
- Symbolic Leadership (Associated with Imparted Meaning)
  - Interprets meanings.
  - Seeks ways to transcend organizational meanings and symbols.
  - Articulates vision or purpose.
  - Strengthens norms.
  - Reinforces culture with traditions or rituals (Johnson, 2014).

Among all these frames and leadership styles the symbolic and political rank most highly in their ability to reveal what was going on during the period of 2000 to 2015. There are reasons for the preeminence of these two frames. Two stand out: (1) critical theory, which we will discuss more fully later, relies heavily upon Marxist analysis which itself is highly politicized, having to do with the organization of pathways over which power flows within a society or an organization; however, Brookfield points out the reluctance of scholars to accept and utilize Marxist tools of analysis as if the collapse of Marxist-based political systems exhausted Marxism's analytical power. He uses the phrase *Marxophobia* to describe this reluctance. In fact:

> If critical theory can be understood as a critical engagement with Marx, then a critical theory of adult learning must begin by acknowledging the centrality of Marxist concepts.
> (Brookfield, 2005, pp. 9, 19, 359)

Also:

> Critical theory has as a priority the critique of capitalism, an ideology viewed by many as coterminous with the best America stands for. Its

intellectual genesis is in Marxism, a fact that is hardly likely to endear it to the vast majority who view Marx as fundamentally un-American ....
it is sometimes stigmatized as a kind of authoritarian, Stalinist creed.
(Brookfield, 2005, p. x)

And: (2) the special place for the symbolic within IHEs; from the structure of the academic departments which mimics that of the medieval guild system, complete with status, prestige, and rank, to commencement, the central liturgy of an IHE, which mirrors the medieval sovereign's court.

Symbolic messages are laden with emotional reactions which carry a deep symbolic resonance. They speak to both the mind and the heart; they focus on how human beings make sense of the chaotic, ambiguous world in which they live (Bolman & Deal, 2013, pp. 243–244).

A unique configuration of power, politics, and critical theory grew adult learning at EC from 2000 to 2015. This configuration most clearly yields its lessons when viewed through the political and symbolic frames; this is not to say the remaining frames are unimportant in the effort to understand this.

Many have had difficulty grasping the full nature of critical theory. What is theory? A theory is a set of understandings that help us make sense of some aspect of the world. Theories may be informal or formal, wider or deeper in scope, and may be expressed in a range of ways, but their basic thrust stays constant – to make sense of the world and to communicate that understanding to others enabling them to take informed action (Brookfield, 2005, pp. 2–3).

How is theory useful? Specifically, how can we judge the utility of a critical theory of adult learning? It is useful to the extent that it provides us with understandings that illuminate what we observe and experience. It helps us name or rename aspects of our experience that elude or puzzle us. It can be an engine that drives our thought beyond an uneasy stasis. Finally, the proper use of critical theory can save us from an energy-sapping, radical pessimism by offering forms of radical hope (Brookfield, 2005, pp. 4–10).

But why critical theory?

> Criticality is a contested idea, one with a variety of meanings, each claimed by different groups for very different purposes.
> (Brookfield, 2005, pp. 10–12)

The concept of criticality is essential to understanding the usefulness of critical theory. It is necessary to unpack this concept to disentangle five constitutional intellectual traditions. These are:

1 Ideology critique like that seen in neo-Marxism.
2 The work of the Frankfurt School of Critical Social Theory (the primary tradition examined in this book).

3 Psychoanalysis, psychotherapy.
4 Analytic philosophy and logic.
5 Pragmatist constructivism.

Out of the school emerged a practical working out of constitutional traditions.

1 Disengagement from assumptions that what is, needs to be.
2 Hegemony which explains why things are as they are.
3 Identification and reappraisal of childhood acquired inhibitions, mostly in the form of traumas.
4 Growth of skilled argument analysis centered on analytic philosophy.
5 Activation of pragmatic constructivism (Brookfield, 2005, pp. 12–16).

There is no single way to tell a story, let alone analyze and interpret it, and I have resisted the temptation to organize this book by such a simple storytelling scheme. This story scheme is far too simple for the content dealt with. Instead, I have imaginatively if somewhat arbitrarily selected certain topics for analysis associated with the growth of adult learning at EC from 2000 to 2015: Part One: Beginnings; Part Two: Accreditation and the CE Plan; Part Three: Faculty; Part Four: Locations; Part Five: Class Conflict; Part Six: Staff; Part Seven: The Rhetoric of Academic Quality. An Introduction and EC Continuing Education Timeline precede these parts; a conclusion follows them.

The additional analytical tool which captures and bolsters some of the foregoing complexity is critical theory with a special emphasis on organizational context rather than on the learner and the learning process. Just how did power, politics, and critical theory combine to grow adult learning and its impact on the organizational context (system) within which adult learning took place at Elizabethtown?

How did they combine to suppress adult learning?

The practice of critical learning theory and its importance have been hard to write about and almost impossible to use as a tool of analysis because:

> In contrast to andragogy and even transformational learning, most practitioners in adult education are unaware of critical theory's potential for examining practice or illuminating the nature of adult learning. This is in part because the writing in this area is dense and obtuse and operationalizing the concepts involved is difficult.
> (Merriam, Caffarella, & Baumgartner, 2007, p. 253)

I seek to show how the learning *system* at EC was directly altered by critical theory's impact.

> The "system" in a critical theory analysis is an institution (such as government or education) that functions to reproduce the status quo, in particular the existing social class structure.
> (Merriam et al., 2007, p. 253)

The systemic impacts of critical theory can, indeed, be skittishly elusive.

Social science intellectuals in Frankfurt, Germany developed the bases of critical theory at the Frankfurt Institute of Social Research. Founded in 1923, the Institute flourished by bringing together men and women who worked at the intersection of philosophy, psychology, and sociology. Hitler and his party closed the institute in 1934. According to Davies (1998, p. 953), the Frankfurt Institute sought:

> a free-floating 'critical theory', conditioned but not determined by the times, (that would impress) a whole generation of social scientists both in the USA and in post-1945 Europe.

Most importantly Influenced by Marx's notion of class conflict, those sheltered by the Frankfurt Institute included: Max Horkheimer, Erich Fromm, Herbert Marcuse, Theodore Adorno, and Jurger Habermas. Its best known research is *Die Dialektik der Aufklarung* (The Dialectic of the Enlightenment) by Horkheimer and Adorno, 1947 (Davies, 1998, p. 953).

Platforms or perspectives for notions of knowledge and truth found in adult education include (these three perspectives have had the greatest impact to date on adult learning):

- Postmodernism
- Feminism
- Critical theory.
(Merriam et al., 2007, pp. 251–253)

The influence of Marx on adult education through critical theory is strong and complicated. The engagement with critical theory is really an engagement with Marx no matter what we may feel about Marxism as a philosophy. This engagement shows itself as a natural skepticism and suspicion of power and an appreciation of the oppressive nature of power relationships (Brookfield, 2005, pp. 19, 97, 105, 195; Merriam et al., 2007, pp. 241–250).

This influence is both direct and indirect; it is found quite openly and less openly in the assumptions that underlie adult educations' programs. Critical theory can be viewed as challenging the adult student as well as the home institution, its administrators, and its faculty with seven transformative tasks:

- Challenging ideology that permeates the environment within which the individual student is called to learn in order to reveal hidden oppression and inequity. Seeks to address embedded injustice.
- Contesting hegemony to foster non-acceptance of an unjust social order.
- Unmasking power to raise awareness of the role various types of power play in our lives and how it is used and abused.
- Overcoming alienation to claim freedom from manipulation. Be a human being and not a thing.
- Learning liberation from the dominant ideology. Seek learning purity.
- Reclaiming reason to broaden its usage in all aspects of life.
- Practicing democracy and learning to live with its contradictions. This process can be messy.

To these seven transformative tasks, I add, due to its growing ubiquity:

- Contesting bureaucratic rationality which promotes a dull form of equality between all things as if learners were interchangeable parts.

These are salient tasks that produce adult citizens who are engaged and active in making the various forms of the human community more humane and better places to live life more fully by challenging the status quo (Merriam et al., 2007, p. 257).

Not only are individual students so challenged, but so are the wider organizations/institutions (social context) that have adult learner programs embedded within them. These wider challenges arise, in part, from the tension that develops when parts of the college or university are tasked to reach out in different ways to different student markets. Additional challenges also arise when those adults who want to learn are exposed to the power of critical theory through their programs, courses, and assignments, as well as through their faculty and administrators. When these adults' expectations arise and grow, failure to meet these expectations results in a gap between the *is* and the *ought* especially as the adult learner attempts to navigate the academic seas of higher education. Thus are created deep-seated, personal and social tensions and challenges. The ability to bridge the *is*/ought gap varies by institution – some are more open to it because of their missions;

others are less open by their failure to translate their missions into more modern relevant verbiage that is market related.

Critical theory operates at three levels: the individual level, learning processes level, and context level. Each of the three levels presents challenges to evaluation and to analysis. In general, though, the first two are more readily analyzed and evaluated than the third; we are drawn, after all, to what is measureable – we can see courses, we can count the credits. Measurement, analysis, and evaluation seem to be more difficult at the third level; perhaps this is so because at the third level we are dealing with more indirect and subtle concepts that probe adult education deeply and:

> Critiques and raises questions about the assumptions we make about the world around us; these assumptions include those underlying the practice of adult education. This ... is called critical, as in critical adult education.
>
> (Merriam et al., 2007, p. 242)

Theoretical astrophysicists have provided us with an enlightening insight that lends support to the use of a powerful analogy:

> just as there is no single theory that explains human learning in general, no single theory of adult learning has emerged to unify the field. Rather, there are a number of theories, models and frameworks, each of which attempts to capture some aspect of adult learning.
>
> (Merriam et al., 2007, p. 103)

This mirrors the astrophysicists' search for the theory of everything – simply and elegantly explaining the big and little things of the universe (Randall, 2015).

And, to the point of the difficulty in identifying the impact of critical theory on the adult learning community:

> Dark matter constitutes 85 percent of the matter in the Universe while ordinary matter – such as that contained in stars, gas, and people – constitutes only 15 percent. Yet people are mainly preoccupied with the existence and relevance of ordinary matter .... However ... it doesn't make sense to focus all our attention on the small percentage .... The dominant 15 percent of matter that we can see and feel is only part of the story .... I will explain dark mater's critical role in the Universe – both for galaxies and for galaxy clusters forming out of the amorphous cosmic plasma in the early Universe – and in maintaining the stability of these structures today.
>
> (Randall, 2015, pp. xiii–xiv)

Again, we readily measure what is readily measureable – like retention and graduation rates that convey important information about the effectiveness of our efforts to mold and shape a certain kind of adult student; yet these visible markers remain a lesser piece of the whole pie. We might borrow Randall's estimation that this visible world constitutes 15% of everything there is. This leaves 85% of critical theory's impact and effects unseen, dark, or at best murky; the major point is that there is more unseen territorial impact than territorial impact that is visible. Still, it is necessary to posit the existence of these invisible impacts in order to explain other observable behaviors. Like the observable fact that there is not enough density at the center of a spiral galaxy to hold all the stars it does in orbit; therefore there must be additional sources of density at work – density or matter that we cannot detect.

Evidence of the impact of power, politics, and critical theory on the institution is easier to find in some cases than in others. Registrar's offices might serve as an example. When presented with the need to run nine accelerated semesters (sessions) per academic year rather than three to support an accelerated degree program for adult learners, these offices are unusually clear in their skepticism and resistance to the change. This skepticism and resistance clash with the high value members of the adult market place on time-to-completion. This type of resistance suppresses adult learning and a refusal to bridge the *is/ought* gap by the institution. This suppression is relatively clear and easy to identify and measure.

On the other hand, an office like financial aid might take a stance on bridging the gap that is much more subtle and nuanced and much more difficult to identify and measure; no small part of this type of response is due to the heavy layers of federal and state regulation that cocoon the activities of this office. There are simply too many regulatory nooks and crannies (or dimensions) that can serve as hiding places for suppression of adult learning. These are difficult to identify and measure. Together, this type of resistance constitutes something like multidimensional cosmological dark matter that is very difficult to see, identify, and measure. The current case study of the development of a successful adult learning program from 2000 to 2015 at EC is replete with examples. It should not be forgotten, however, that each part of a small college or university operates within a unique environment that can profoundly affect its responses. It should also be remembered that even though these examples, in effect, suppressed the growth of adult learning, their reversal could foster the growth of adult learning. That was the effect in these particular examples.

Using critical theory as an analytical tool arising with the individual adult learner and the learning process, but applied at the institutional (context) level, we find adult education units challenging the wider college or university in all eight areas listed above. These challenges disrupt the familiar pathways of power, politics, and learning theories. Most of these important challenges and disruptions occur in the murkiness of the invisible world, but:

> Power is always alterable and disruptive.
> (Merriam et al., 2007, p. 249)

Discussions of critical theory's challenges to ideology, contesting hegemony, unmasking power, overcoming alienation, learning liberation, reclaiming reason, practicing democracy, and contesting bureaucratic rationality, most likely use the rhetoric of academic quality. How can subject content be taught in accelerated formats? How can student engagement occur in online courses and/or programs? How can a faculty whose employment status is part-time deliver the same quality learning experiences delivered by full-time, tenured faculty? How qualified are adults who have been out of college or university for many years in mastering higher learning? I have experienced over 20 years of this type of engagement with colleagues at traditional, residential colleges and I am impressed by the diversity of arguments over the quality of adult learning programs. I am also impressed by the real opportunities these encounters provide to discuss the organization-wide issues like: what is academic quality, what constitutes good learning? However, in most cases if you strip away the rhetorical mask of academic quality (one of the primary tasks of critical theory), you will more than likely find that these arguments are essentially political and have to do with the legitimization of power and those who exercise it. Who owns the curricula? Who controls learning? Who determines what should be learned? Who is a member of the faculty? What does shared governance mean? How does part-time employment status impact governance? Where does power come from and how does it flow? These questions do not present themselves with the clarity of those that deal with academic quality; indeed, they are difficult to identify, let alone answer, because, as important as they are, they reside on the dark side of critical theory's impact. Still, they make up a status quo or ideological background that we can assume lies behind all else.

The budgeting processes of the small university or college provide other examples of arguments and decisions that bubble up from the darker world of critical impacts. One such example concerns arguments and decisions about where to record the revenue and expenses generated by adult learning programs. How one answers this question is important. One certainly wants an accounting of revenues and expenses detailed enough to present a true picture of the program's financial health. But where is this recorded in the macro-budget? Many place this data under auxiliary activities: along with the bookstore, dining services, etc. Others integrate this data with the single, generalized categories like instruction, direct cost of instruction, indirect cost of instruction, etc. The first placement connotes it is not academically generated revenue/expenses; the second connotes that it is. The first treats the adult learner as a second class academic student, whose revenue/expenses are treated similarly to those generated by the sale of a cheeseburger at the student union. At EC, it took two years of concerted effort by me and the provost/senior vice-president to move our adult learner revenue in such a way as to not connote second class student status. The pervasiveness of such a distinction can be very wide and can be bolstered by decisions that may seem to have very little to do with it. Yet the message is clear and it is a negative one if you happen to fall into the second class category. While denials by the financial side of the house that any such categorization takes place, the evidence suggests that it does and it can serve as a mode of suppression of adult learning if those programs and their financials are treated as second class.

The second class categorization of adult learning programs and their students is not always obvious but it is ubiquitous throughout the larger institution housing these programs and students. And once again the rhetoric of academic quality is used to suppress adult learning programs. The attitude of the EC student newspaper, the *Etownian*, is a clear example. In the midst of an intra-institutional political struggle over who should develop and implement a new MBA program – the business department or the School for Continuing and Professional Studies (SCPS) – the *Etownian* asserted that the mere presence of adult learners on campus watered down the degree and that these adult learners should be invited to leave the college. This type of attack was notable for its viciousness and resulted in at least one adult student leaving the classroom in tears. The message was clear: adult learners were second class learners at EC. The *Etownian*'s arguments closely mirrored those advanced by the business department. This attempt at suppression of adult learning at EC should have been answered by the president or the provost/senior vice president. There was nothing but silence from those quarters, however. And, finally, as dean of the SCPS, I responded to it. So what was this really about? Did adult learners really devalue the EC degree? Or who had the power to admit students and to set standards for the admission? Clearly, the real issue was a political one put forth under the guise of student/academic quality. A reader unfamiliar with the issue would see only the academic rhetoric; others might view the article through the political frame.

Still, those who work in adult learning and with the adults doing the learning are hardly blameless for this dual class system (context/organization).

We do, after all, insist that adult learners be recognized as discrete, self-conscious learners with needs and desires specific to their position or stage of life. We have done a lot to raise the self-awareness of this group; what results is something like class consciousness. In the end, we who work in adult learning, carry a great deal of responsibility for insisting on treatment that supports a dual-class system throughout higher education. We should look at this and weigh advantage or disadvantage.

So, these events, when viewed through our analytical framework, take on a shadowy kind of politically powerful suppression of adult learning at EC. A suppression not immediately visible as such.

Our chosen analytical tools – the frames from *Reframing Organizations* and critical theory applied to organizational context – illuminate the darker organizational corners where suppression of adult learning lurks.

It's wise not to underestimate the analytical power of the frames; Bolman and Deal are safe in concluding:

> As organizations have become pervasive and dominant, they have also become harder to understand and manage. The result is that managers are often nearly as clueless as their subordinates – the Dilberts of the world – think they are. The consequences of myopic management and leadership show up every day, sometimes in small and subtle ways, sometimes in catastrophes. Our basic premise is that a primary cause of managerial failure is faulty thinking rooted in inadequate ideas. Managers and those who try to help them too often rely on narrow models that capture only part of organizational life.
>
> Learning multiple perspectives, or frames, is a defense against thrashing around without a clue about what you are doing or why. Frames serve multiple functions. They are filters for sorting essence from trivia, maps that aid navigation, and tools for solving problems and getting things done. This book is organized around four frames rooted in both managerial wisdom and social science knowledge. The structural approach focuses on the architecture of organization – the design of units and subunits, rules and roles, goals and policies. The human resource lens emphasizes understanding people – their strengths and foibles, reason and emotion, desires and fears. The political view sees organizations as competitive arenas of scarce resources, competing interests, and struggles for power and advantage. Finally the symbolic frame focuses on issues of meaning and faith. It puts ritual, ceremony, story, play, and culture at the heart of organizational life.
>
> Each of the frames is powerful and coherent. Collectively they make it possible to reframe, looking at the same thing from multiple lenses or points of view. When the world seems hopelessly confusing and

nothing is working, reframing is a powerful tool for gaining clarity, regaining balance, generating new options, and finding strategies that make a difference.

(Bolman & Deal, 2013, pp. 20–22)

What follows this introduction is a *Timeline of Continuing Education at Elizabethtown College.* Certain issues and conflicts during that 116-year history I have labeled critical. The chapters that follow this timeline deal, in one way or another, with these critical issues, observe them, analyze them, and suggest some takeaways/recommendations for the reader. So, the contributions of each chapter and the book as a whole form a mix of the theoretical, analytical, and practical. The reader is urged to select what is useful for her purposes. This scheme supports the interrelated nature of all three levels and suggests that an understanding of all three is required to grasp the state of adult learning in higher education today.

2 Continuing Education Timeline at Elizabethtown College 1899–2014

The following traces the development of Continuing Education's (CE) adult outreach at Elizabethtown College (EC) in Elizabethtown, Pennsylvania. In 1951, the college responded to demobilization and the GI bill; in 1972, the college responded to the growing community college movement. These are just two of the most prominent examples of EC's persistent efforts to reach the adult learner. Under the headings Critical Conflicts/Issues, I have identified specific conflicts/issues that most often made up particularly durable facades covering the power relationships behind them; these relationships present a truer face of critical theory's impact on the institutional context of adult learning. Many of the timeline examples of this nature, reveal the true nature of powerful, political relationships at the college such as where they are and who comprises them. What often emerges is an alternating pattern of suppression and/or nurturance of adult learning.

This timeline also serves as one simple mechanism of organization of the book's content.

Something like a practical checklist can be coaxed from this timeline. With this in mind, I urge the reader to reflect upon what worked at EC and whether it might enlighten what is going on at their institution of higher education (IHE) and/or how these practicalities might be applied within their own IHE if appropriate. The fit will never be perfect, but it may be helpful.

The timeline works at three levels: (1) as an illuminator of darker, more hidden issues and their impacts; (2) as a simple but effective organizational principle by which the book can be organized; and (3) as a checklist providing valuable insights for understanding how power, politics, and critical theory operate at the readers' IHE in relation to adult learning.

Highlights

1899 – EC was founded by members of the Church of the Brethren, one of three historic peace churches. Today, the college is a private liberal arts institution of higher education with approximately 2,700 students – 1,800 primarily residential students, 800 adult part-time students, and about 100 part-time graduate students.

1900 – First classes were offered in Elizabethtown, Pennsylvania.

1921 – Formal accreditation was granted by the Pennsylvania Department of Public Instruction.

1948 – Formal accreditation was granted by the Middle States Association of Colleges and Secondary Schools, the college's major regional accrediting organization.

1951 – Harrisburg Area College Center was established between EC and Lebanon Valley College to provide afternoon and evening classes to adults.

1966 – The center was renamed University Center at Harrisburg. Temple University, Penn State University, and the University of Pennsylvania joined the program.

1970 – Community Congress (CC) was approved by Board of Trustees (BOT).

1972 – The Center for Community Education (CCE) was established as a separate college unit under the oversight of the CC.

1980s and 1990s – New academic programs were added.

1986 – CC was abolished by the college president and the BOT.

1990 – The Institute for Learning in Retirement was launched, providing credit-free courses for an older population.

1993 – The Church of the Brethren gave up direct governance role and was replaced by an independent BOT.

2001 – The center was renamed the Center for Continuing Education and Distance Learning (CCEDL); accelerated course format began; accelerated online courses were introduced.

2003 – Elizabethtown partnered with F&M College to offer classes in downtown Lancaster.

2004 – Weekend intensive classes were offered for the first time; intense educational experience structured around a Friday, Saturday, and Sunday core.

2006 – The James B. Hoover Center for Business was opened.

2009 – The York Center opened at St Charles Way. It had very corporate optics.

2010 – The first fully online majors were offered.

2011 – CCEDL received the 2011 Excellence in Innovation Award from the National Council for Accelerated Programs (CAP).

2012 – The MBA program was established; the first separate CCEDL commencement ceremony was held.

2013 – The center was renamed Elizabethtown College School of Continuing and Professional Studies (SCPS).

Beyond the Highlights

1921

Formal accreditation was granted by the Pennsylvania Department of Public Instruction.

1948

Formal accreditation was granted by the Middle States Association of Colleges and Secondary Schools. This was and still is EC's main regional accrediting body.

1951

EC and Lebanon Valley Colleges (LVC) established the Harrisburg Pennsylvania Area College Center, providing college-level classes in the afternoon and evening for adult students in the Harrisburg area. The scheduled times of classes expanded accessibility for adults. Classes were first held in the Central High School Building in Harrisburg and credits could be applied toward a degree at either Elizabethtown or LVC.

Mission of EC

Molded by a commitment to educate for service, EC is a community of learners dedicated to educating students intellectually, socially, aesthetically, and ethically for lives of service and leadership as citizens of the world. As a comprehensive institution, the college offers academic programs in the liberal arts, sciences, and professional studies. Combining classroom instruction with experiential learning these programs advance independent thought, personal integrity, and social responsibility as the foundations of a life of learning. Founded by members of the Church of the Brethren, the college believes that learning is most noble when used to benefit others and affirms the values of peace, non-violence, human dignity, and social justice.

Critical Conflicts/Issues

Note the overlap between the values of EC's Mission Statement and those of the eight transformative tasks of critical theory for adult learning. In a small step toward challenging ideology, accessibility to college classes was enhanced by offering classes in the evenings or late afternoon as opposed to daytime classes only.

1966

The joint venture succeeded and Temple University, Penn State University, and the University of Pennsylvania joined the program so that the center was able to offer graduate work as well as undergraduate work. Robert A. Byerly, a professor of religion at EC, was the center's first director, and A.C. Baugher was the first chairman of the board. In 1966 the name was changed to the University Center at Harrisburg, and by the end of the 1960s an average semester had an enrollment of up to 1,500 students and a six-acre campus complete with classroom building, offices, and a library. The location still flourishes today as Dixon University Center. It is part of the State System of Higher Education (PASSHE) and EC continues to offer classes there.

Critical Conflicts/Issues

The level of trust and respect between the participating institutions was remarkable.

Each accepted the others' credits toward the completion of degrees; the true beneficiaries were the thousands of students who otherwise would have been denied access to quality higher education because of scheduled class time.

Liberal transfer credit evaluation was introduced – less aging of credits, etc.; more open and liberal attitudes guided the transfer of previous credit protocols. This reduced time to completion and reduced financial responsibilities for degree completion.

Courses and credits could be applied to any member institution's degree programs.

There was free flow of educational goods and services between institutions.

Status and prestige were less important than they are today when they are used to create a rankings system that builds walls and obstacles between institutions rather than facilitate the free exchange of educational goods and services.

1970

Five hundred students petitioned the President for a new, more democratic, governance body. The BOT approved the new CC in April 1970.

1972

The college established the CCE as an autonomous, self-governing unit to provide educational opportunities for adults, professional retirees, and other students who were not able to participate in the college's residential programming. The mission of the center was to extend the boundaries of the college's learning community to include a wider and more diverse population, thereby mutually enriching the institution and the community. In more recent times, the continuing education (CE) unit at the college was still guided by the belief that learning is lifelong and most noble when used to benefit others (Williamson, 2001, pp. 259, 269, 275, 290–292).

Critical Conflicts/Issues

EC's flat, democratic governing body, the CC created the CCE in 1972 in response, in part, to the Community College Movement. Power flowed much more horizontally over the CC's pathways than more typical, more vertical structuring; practicing democracy, one of the eight transformative tasks of critical theory is evident here. Such a practice would prove to be messy.

The CC was comprised of four academic divisions, a student division and a division for administrators. Voting was on an equal basis and administrative and academic questions were thrown open to all groups. A truly democratic structure, human resources, the politics, and the symbolic.

New programs and majors were added with the goal of continually addressing the needs of working adults. The center's programs were innovative for the time. They recognized the unique qualities and experiences that adult learners bring with them into the academic environment. An early example of the college's support for the value of experiential learning is the EXCEL Program (known at its inception as the Adult External Degree Program, or AEDP), a degree completion program that has, at its foundation, the recognition of real-world learning as worthy of academic credit based on a portfolio protocol. This program is still in existence today and the concept of experiential/real-world learning has become part of more commonly accepted practice in higher education.

1980s

The center joined the Institute for Learning in Retirement (ILR), a program committed to offering lifelong learning opportunities to older adults in the community. Each semester, a series of classes was offered in subject areas such as politics, computer and internet technology, history, biographies, sciences, art, and religion. There were no tests nor grades. Classes were held during the day at the main campus and at various local senior citizens' communities. All programs were non-credit. The classes were taught by college faculty and staff as well as experts from the community. Trips to places of cultural interest were offered as well.

Critical Conflicts/Issues

By the 1980s, the CCE and especially its autonomy were under full-time faculty and administrative attack. As usual the rhetoric of the attack was that of academic quality – open admissions, college credit for life experiences, liberal credit transfer evaluation. Thus, the CCE was brought under traditional hierarchical oversight – by full-time faculty and administrators. This rhetoric masked the underlying power relationships at work; it was these relationships that mattered, not the masks that covered them.

1986

With the support of the president, the BOT abolished the CC. The CCE and its structures persisted but were brought under more usual hierarchical oversight; this structural change smothered innovation.

There was a failure of internal marketing to bring faculty and administrators along to a fuller understanding of and support for the CCE.

1990s

The center added two new majors as well as additional non-credit programming for realtors, accountants, and social workers. By the end of the 1990s, less than 98 non-traditional learners were generating revenue for the college through credit, degree-completion credit (most revenue generating credit was degree-completion credit), and non-credit programs and classes. Financially, the center showed a ($5,000) loss; its first loss in many years.

Critical Conflict/Issues

A steady attrition in the number of non-traditional students and a major slowdown of revenue from the resources housed in the CCE occurred, as CCE lost its innovative basis and autonomy and the ability to serve its markets. This slowdown affected the college-wide budget.

1998

A new EC strategic plan recognized the pressing need to recommit EC to continuing education efforts in order to increase the number of non-traditional learners participating in the life of the college. The plan utilized the language of diversity and revenues.

Critical Conflicts/Issues

The goals of the 1998 strategic plan were noteworthy; yet, the language of the document was unclear and contradictory. Autonomy and CCE self-governance, keys to CCE success, were downplayed and to be avoided. Preservation of the familiar pathways of power took priority over a CCE structure proven to produce results.

2000

Students from Japan's Nihon University first came to EC for intensive language study in the summer of 2000. The center provided administrative support for the directors of the program who came from the modern languages department of the college.

A new dean of continuing education was hired with a clear charge to increase the number of non-traditional students (matriculated students and revenue flow). The center was renamed the Center for Continuing Education and Distance Learning. (CCEDL) The Council of Academic Management (CAM) was established to govern the center academically and administratively. CAM members were from the CCEDL faculty, the adult learners, alumni, the community, and administrative groups. This body worked well and could move quickly and flexibly on issues and program approvals. Items requiring trustee approval could move quickly to that body for final approval; at its largest, the CAM had a membership of only 15. In addition, meetings were conducted with appropriate infrastructure groups to discuss the impact of this movement toward autonomy. This was an arduous process and the result was undergraduate accelerated degree- completion. Despite the language of the 1998 strategic plan, the CCEDL was largely autonomous and self-governing under a new CE revitalization plan.

Critical Conflicts/Issues

- Transfer Credit Evaluation by appropriate standards that benefit the adult learner.
- Movement from fifteen-week semesters to five-week sessions with twenty contact hours in class.
- Courses taught according to learning modules which were standardized and which were strongly based on clearly articulated learning outcomes with built in assessment metrics.

Faculty were part-time employees of the college/CCEDL. Other duties beyond facilitation were distinctly bundled; when these bundles were opened and their tasks undertaken by faculty, faculty was compensated by the task performed. These tasks included:

- Learning Module writing.
- Facilitation of classroom content.
- Service as lead facilitators (serve like department chairs).
- Learning module revisions.
- Service on curriculum review teams.
- Facilitation of learning, not mere teaching of learning.
- Attendance of at least two faculty developments a year.
- Financial aid adjustments.
- College's first online classes.

As the CCEDL dean, I made a personal presentation to the traditional College's Faculty Assembly; there were no questions when the floor opened. Yet within a week, five faculty members from the business department had signed a letter, expressing their dismay at allowing access to "unqualified students", and how their mere presence in the classroom would lower quality for all students, devaluing the college's education. It was a blatant example of intellectual arrogance. The matter was deftly and effectively handled by the Provost/Dean of Faculty.

CCEDL added a criminal justice major to its array of programs. Development of this major served as somewhat of a model for later programs. The administrative team worked with a taskforce of experts working in the field (chiefs-of-police), court personnel, and even the future commissioner of the Pennsylvania State Police. Other programs tried to follow this developmental model, especially at the graduate level.

2003

EC partnered with F & M College in Lancaster to offer its accelerated degree programs on the campus of F&M; adult learners could, thereby, complete their EC degree right in their own community. CCEDL utilized F&M classrooms, library, and bookstore services in return for a percentage of net tuition revenue. It provided its own admissions and professional academic advising. One way to keep enrollments and revenues on the upward curve is to open new locations. It is not guaranteed but in general holds true. This was a very unique approach to the structuring of locations usually found associated with community colleges.

Critical Conflicts/Issues

How would this model differ from others such as Dixon University? What would the impact of a third party have on the process of opening a new location? Would that impact be positive or negative?

How should we approach college personnel who are already well versed in Dixon University processes?

2004

The CCEDL began administering the Noel Levitz Adult Learner Inventory (ALI) to our adult learners on an annual basis to measure student satisfaction and the importance students assigned to eight different scales of adult learning effectiveness. The inventory allowed for comparisons to national norms for each administration. CCEDL students reported high levels of satisfaction, consistently beating national norms. Year to year comparisons were very helpful in isolating specific problem areas.

Weekend intensives were initiated as a new delivery format. This addition enhanced the sessions available to CCEDL students and thereby enhanced accessibility.

Critical Conflicts/Issues

This year the president of the college invited the dean of the CCEDL to join his senior staff.

2006

On September 14, the college celebrated the opening and dedication of the James B. Hoover Center for Business. Among other achievements, the day celebrated three individuals who made the $5.2 million building possible – S. Dale High of Lancaster, James B. Hoover of Locus Valley, NY, and Edward R. Murphy of Lynbrook, NY.

The center found a new home in the Hoover Center through the generous support of Edward R. Murphy. This home provided a professional, up-to-date, and modern environment in classrooms and administrative offices.

2009

The center expanded its outreach by opening the York center. CCEDL also signed an agreement with HACC to deliver its business administration degree at HACC-York.

The Charlotte W. Newcomb Foundation awarded a grant to the center to establish an endowed scholarship to support bachelor's degree-seeking students 25 years old or older.

Middle States' Association of Colleges and Secondary Schools visited and reaccredited the college. It commended the CCEDL for its rigorous programming and its assessment of learning outcomes. It held the CCEDL model up for emulation by the traditional College.

2010

The center added its first fully online majors: Human Services, Human Services (Behavioral and Addictions Counseling), and Business Administration. Credits generated through online registrations grew rapidly until they constituted over 60% of total registrations by 2015.

2011

The National Council for Accelerated Programs (CAP) awarded the CCEDL, its 2011 Excellence in Innovation Award. This award from this prestigious organization recognized the center at Elizabethtown for innovation in the areas of overall governance and structure, admissions and marketing, programs and delivery features, standards and assessments, and faculty development.

Plans for an MBA through the center raised the ire of the traditional business department, culminating at the trustees' meeting. The issues revolved around requirements for AACSB (Association to Advance Collegiate Schools of Business) accreditation. The trustees voted in favor of the CCEDL MBA. A residue of ill feeling on all sides remained. The support of the provost/senior vice president was key in moving on from this hostile status.

Critical Conflicts/Issues

The move of the dean to senior staff was a major event that elevated the credibility and legitimacy of the CCEDL. This movement did a lot to entrench those characteristics that were responsible for the organization's success with its markets. It was also a victory for the adult learner who now had direct access to the top of the college hierarchy. There was a downside to this event, however; it sharpened the lines of division with those who opposed EC's adult learner outreach. But even this negative helped clarify issues in a positive way.

2012

The MBA program started in January, with classes offered in Harrisburg and Lancaster.

May 19 was the first time the college held a separate commencement for CCEDL graduates. One hundred and three graduates walked on stage to accept their EC degree. Again, any resentment caused by this change helped clarify issues and advanced the discussion of the role of adult learners in the life of the college.

This year the center established the Chi Epsilon Chapter of Alpha Sigma Lambda Honor Society for adult learners.

Critical Conflicts/Issues

EC was identified by Dr. Carol Kasworm, a major scholar of adult education, as a case exemplar and served as such in HEAD –Case Study for HEAD—Opening Higher Education to Adults, a report for the European Commission of the European Union.

2014–2015

A Master of Science in Leadership (MSL) was developed and implemented.

Critical Conflicts/Issues

The Edward R. Murphy Center for Continuing Education and Distance Learning (CCEDL) became the Elizabethtown College School of Continuing and Professional Studies. (SCPS) This change affirmed the important role adult learners have and will continue to have in higher education at Elizabethtown.

As of 2015, the SCPS served over 800 matriculated undergraduate adult learners and nearly 100 matriculated graduate adult learners. These students were served at six locations in the region and produced over $6 million in revenue each year. Between 60% and 70% of all course registrations were completely online.

SCPS Mission

EC's SCPS seeks to extend the boundaries of the college's learning community to include a wider and more diverse population. The school expresses the values of the college's mission through a commitment to and advocacy of degree and non-degree academic programs for adult learners. In particular, the school embraces the values of human dignity and social justice by widening access to quality higher education for adults. In its programs and outreach, the school fosters a learner-centered academic culture that expresses the college's belief that learning is lifelong and most noble when used to benefit others.

Part One
Beginnings

> Yahweh God planted a garden in Eden which is in the East, and there he put the man he had fashioned. Yahweh God caused to spring up from the soil every kind of tree, enticing to look at and good to eat, with the tree of life and the tree of the knowledge of good and evil in the middle of the garden.
>
> (Genesis 2:8–10)

3 Partnerships in Adult Education and the Impact of Critical Theory

In 1951 Elizabethtown College (EC) and Lebanon Valley College (LVC) established the Harrisburg Pennsylvania Area College Center, providing college-level classes in the afternoon and evening for adult learners; classes were held in the Central High School building in Harrisburg and credits could be applied toward a degree at either EC or LVC. This outreach was an attempt by these colleges to meet the higher educational needs of thousands of Second World War demobilized veterans who could take advantage of the new GI Bill of educational rights and funding; this market was adult in nature, whether defined simply chronologically or by personal characteristics of economic independence and responsibility. Definitions of who is an adult student tend to vary. This outreach expressed itself mainly through the scheduling of classes at the times these adults could attend; although far from flashy, this fact should not be underestimated in its impact in making higher education more accessible to this group. In its small way, the move to more accessible class times challenged the prevalent ideology of when the right time for classes to be held was. The challenge attached itself to the structure of the program. However, there apparently was little effort to explore the larger questions and issues of what it would mean to bring curricula and faculty into more adult orientations, implementations, and engagements. New scheduling of classes may have been a small step but it at least opened the door to a consideration of these larger questions and issues.

This joint venture at Harrisburg, Pennsylvania, spearheaded by two small, independent liberal education colleges, was so successful that Temple University, Penn State University, and the University of Pennsylvania were eager to lend their names to it and joined the program. The venture's success indicated that there was a clear-cut need. In 1966, the name was changed to the University Center at Harrisburg; by the end of the 1960s an average semester had an enrollment of up to 1,500 students; the university center rested on a six-acre campus. It still flourishes today as the *Dixon*

University Center. It is part of the Pennsylvania State System of Higher Education (PASSHE); today EC is joined by ten other institutions of higher education (IHEs): Bloomsburg University, Environmental Training Institute (University of Texas at Arlington), Evangelical Seminary, Immaculata University, IUP (Indiana University of Pennsylvania), Lebanon Valley College, Lock Haven University, Millersville University, Rochester Institute of Technology, and Shippensburg University. The outreach was definitely aimed at adults. The venture was best described as an academic consortium. EC currently dominates undergraduate accelerated offerings but also offers several graduate programs at Harrisburg. Arguably, EC's offerings are the most innovative. Dixon University Center invests in marketing to better understand the adult market it serves; this modifies the program as strictly an academic consortium by providing this financial dimension. There is also an attempt to protect current members from direct competition with other members. By the late 1960s, however, status and prestige as bases for evaluative rankings of IHEs were surging and were strong enough that truly innovative practices that benefited the adult learner were strait-jacketed and the free exchange of credits, majors, and degrees was corralled.

Observations/Analysis

Anyone who has worked on collaborative ventures between or among colleges and universities can attest to the Eden-like quality of the collaborative in Harrisburg founded in the early 1950s; the level of trust and respect between participating institutions was quite remarkable. Each accepted the others' credits for the completion of a degree. The true beneficiaries, of course, were the adult learners who otherwise would have been denied access to quality higher education. And liberal transfer credit evaluations saved the student money.

With only the slightest of exaggeration, what happened at Harrisburg, Pennsylvania in the early 1950s was truly notable. The structural, human resources, political, and symbolic frames showed themselves to be remarkably flexible and porous; they formed doorways that allowed for a liberal exchange between schools of higher educational products like courses, programs, and degrees.

Critical theory operated at a relatively low level focused on a simple but salient structural change (scheduling of classes). Also of some importance, is how critical theory attached itself to the structure of the adult education system or organization. Indeed, the result was to uplift and nourish adult learning by the system rather than to suppress it.

It should be noted that the role of status and prestige among the member institutions was muted in the 1950s which allowed a level of collaboration and cooperation otherwise unattainable. This was a persistent theme between and among these local IHEs. As the rankings movement grew after the early 1950s, it set a premium on competition and separation that dampened cooperative efforts and the free exchange of educational goods.

Takeaways

Most colleges and universities today operate within an evaluative context defined by status and prestige which preclude the free exchange of higher educational goods we saw at Harrisburg in the 1950s. Still, Harrisburg's lessons provide guidelines to establishing effective adult outreach today. These guidelines include:

- Seek the most porous and flexible frames on which to build your adult learning outreach. These will vary by each institution's unique characteristics and mission.
- Let good will drive the outreach efforts for as long as possible. Assume you have the support you need to be effective until shown otherwise. Assume non-competitive principles that underlie your actions. This is a difficult guideline to follow with lots of room for a diversity of applications.
- Remember that your institution is most probably a runner in the race for status and prestige and, as critical theory informs us, the system will defend this as status quo. The challenge is to find ways around this defense. Only very rarely will head-on confrontation get you where you want to go. Be clever.
- In your own institution's history, seek programs that exhibited the qualities you are seeking – if you find them, hold them up as models to be emulated. Use the historical dimension to bolster your arguments.

4 Critical Theory's Structural Democratic Impulse

In the wake of what can only be called a democratic tsunami, Elizabethtown College (EC) in 1970 established the Community Congress (CC) to govern the college. The president was moved by a petition signed by 500 students asking for this change. The CC was made up of four academic divisions, a student division, and an administrative group. Most democratically, students, administrators, and faculty shared voting membership. The CC was empowered to make all academic, professional, and social policies subject to review and approval by the trustees (Williamson, 2001, p. 259). The proposed constitution of the CC was ratified by the student association and the administrator group in March of 1970 and by the trustees in April 1970.

The Center for Community Education (CCE) was the child of the CC; the CCE was an autonomous, self- governing unit charged with providing educational opportunities for adults, professional retirees, and other students who were not able to participate in the college's residential programming. In large part, the CCE was a response to the growing community college movement. The mission of the CCE was to extend the boundaries of the college's learning community to include a wider and more diverse population, thereby mutually enriching the institution and the community. The CCE was approved by the Board of Trustees (BOT) as a unit separate from the residential college in 1972. It was a unit with the charge of offering open-university type programs.

The CC and the trustees empowered the CCE to offer any and all degrees EC was authorized to offer. The CCE could also develop new majors; and could identify, develop, employ, fire, and hire its own faculty.

Observations/Analysis

A hearty strain of democracy flowered at EC in 1972. Its main governance body was the CC which included administrators and students as well as representatives from four academic areas. The final say rested with the BOT. Both the CC and the trustees approved the creation of the CCE. Diplomas were issued in the name of the CCE.

Both the CC and its creation, the CCE, reflected the growing attractiveness of critical theory to the structures at Elizabethtown configured to form an adult education learning community. This constituted a robust outbreak and application of critical theory's challenge to the status quo. As such, we find here examples of challenging ideology and practicing democracy. The CCE programs were very innovative; they recognized the unique qualities and experiences that adult learners bring with them into academic environments. An example of EC's support for experiential learning was the Adult External Degree Program (AEDP), a degree-completion program that has, as its basis, real-world learning. This program was still in existence as of 2015 by which time the concept of experiential/real-world learning had become a larger part of accepted practice in higher education and even a mark of educational excellence for an institution. The program is known as the EXCEL program today.

Both the democratic approval protocol of the CCE and its enumerated powers and structure, affirmed EC's leadership in higher education innovation, especially adult learning innovation, as well as a blending of structural, human resources, political, and symbolic frames of reference.

The origin of these CCE characteristics is found in the adult learning outreach of the early 1950s. This period opened the door for critical theory to penetrate the power and politics of EC, the result being the CCE of 1972. But there is another source that should be considered and that source includes the democratic impulses of EC's founding denomination – the Church of the Brethren. This democratic and egalitarian milieu was a rich source of nourishment for innovation in adult outreach – the tasks of critical learning theory energized the entire system – in this case, in a positive, visible way. The Church of the Brethren is also one of three traditional Peace Churches along with the Mennonites and Quakers. The denomination emphasized the moral autonomy and responsibility of the individual over the group. The CC was an expression of these values; standing out and above the group could be deemed almost unchristian. Even though the Church of the Brethren relinquished formal governance functions of the college in 1993, a cultural residue of Brethren values was and is still strong at EC.

To these particular institutional characteristics should more general and widespread democracy-driven characteristics be added. The 1960s and 1970s were a chaotic time of change that nourished things democratic. This wider democratic milieu played its own role in practicing democracy. Led by opposition to the Vietnam War, a host of democratic expressions peppered the decades – mass demonstrations, teach-ins, pass/fail protocols among them.

From the early 1950s to the 1970s, power and politics worked to support the growth of adult learning, due to the attachment of elements of critical theory to the structure of the adult learning community.

Takeaways

- The dimension of time is one that is often neglected when using the four frames of analysis. Look beyond the present and into the past to see how any of the four frames were used and how they developed. It needn't be a perfect fit. Examples of partial analysis and critical learning theory can usually be found through careful searching. Use what is found as the basis for building new, adult learning programs. It is hard to argue against an innovation that is a tradition as well.
- Look for the places and times where critical theory brilliantly and explicitly shaped programs and impacted them at all three levels – individual, process, and systemic context. Use this brilliance to light the path ahead for yourself and others.

5 Challenges to the Status Quo

By the mid-1980s, a coalition of EC administrators and full-time faculty politically attacked the Community Congress (CC) and the Center for Community Education (CCE). The president of the college pursued a policy of increasing status and prestige and the resultant higher rankings for the college; he established the premise that the CC, led by CCE's programming, was not the type a high prestige college or university should pursue; this adult outreach was positively hurtful to EC's status and prestige and thus, its rankings among other institutions of higher education. Again, the language of the opposition was the rhetoric of academic quality – open admissions, college credits for life experiences, liberal transfer credit evaluation, accelerated formats, and use of part-time faculty, as well as lack of effectiveness. The alternate adult learning community established by the CC and the CCE had overstepped its bounds. The proper place for the functions that fell outside those proper bounds was with the faculty and administration. The Board of Trustees (BOT) abolished the CC in October 1986. The structure of the CCE persisted, however, stripped of its power, and was brought firmly under the administrative oversight of the provost/dean of faculty; it lost its autonomy and with that loss came a loss in the CCE's ability to meet the needs of the adult learner. By the 1990s fewer than 98 non-traditional learners were generating revenue for the college through degree-completion programs. This steady attrition of enrollments and revenue from CCE in-house resources meant the CCE was losing its innovative orientation. The center showed a $5,000 loss in the 1990s. This affected the college-wide budget. (Williamson, 2001, pp. 290–291).

Observations/Analysis

The CCE was born of truly democratic governance under the CC; it valued real-world experience as well as classroom earned credits. The CC and CCE were targets of the powerful relationships and the politics that underlay the structural, human resources, political, and symbolic frames, especially the latter two. CCE challenged, contested, and democratized. In so doing, it was anti-hegemonic and represented an opportunity for the unmasking of true power relationships and goals. The administrative and faculty coalition effectively suppressed adult learning at EC.

Best understood through the political and symbolic frames, the rhetoric of the discussion was again that of academic quality. Beneath the academic debates was a strong political process at work. EC could not tolerate an independent in-house rival to the traditional program. In the CCE, EC faced a very pure form of critical theory at work. The real debate was about who controlled learning at EC – behind all the academic rhetoric, critical theory was operating quite openly. And, with a nice Marxist twist, it gave rise to the very reactionary forces that suppressed it.

Takeaways

- Realize that in most cases powerful political realities lay behind the academic rhetoric of quality. These powerful political realities sought the suppression of adult learning and its programs because of the threat they posed to the dominant ideology and hegemony. Do not fall victim to Marxophobia; do not fear looking beneath the surface.
- The political and symbolic frames were the preeminent frames at work – the symbolic because it captured the college's perception of its own identity.
- Critical theory's impact on systemic context threatened powerful stakeholder groups dedicated to preserving the status quo. In this case these stakeholders triumphed.

Part Two
Accreditation and the Continuing Education Plan

> The tree of liberty must be refreshed from time to time with the blood of patriots and tyrants.
>
> (Thomas Jefferson)

6 Self-Studies
1998 and 2009

In 1999, Elizabethtown College (EC) tried to address what had become a very anemic adult outreach. This attempt appears in the college's 1999 self-study for reaccreditation by Middle States Commission on Higher Education (MSCHE), EC's regional accrediting agency. It also appears in the EC Strategic Plan of 1998. Recommendations called for a working plan to revitalize the Community Education (CE) program over the next five years. Any plan had to integrate CE programs with the mainstream academic programs and must have the support and involvement of full- time faculty and departments.

Thus, the self-study opines:

> nontraditional students currently make up a very small percentage of our overall student population. Nonetheless... most academic departments are very receptive to nontraditional students and some have programs that could easily accommodate their needs.
> (Elizabethtown College Ten Year Self-Study for Middle States Commission on Higher Education, 1999, p. 29)
>
> The Strategic Plan identifies the revival of Continuing Education and recruitment of nontraditional students as important initiatives that can strengthen the learning community. An organized and thoughtful plan needs to be developed to optimize these possibilities.
> (Elizabethtown College Self-Study Committee, 1999, pp. 29–30)

The self-study recommended:

> Evaluate the existing Continuing Education programs and develop a working plan for revitalizing this program over the next five years. This plan must effectively integrate CE programs with the mainstream

academic programs and must have support and involvement of full-time faculty and departments.
(Elizabethtown College Self-Study Committee, 1999, p. 50)

Approximately ten years later, much had changed, including the name of the continuing education unit. The name was changed to the Center for Continuing Education and Distance Learning (CCEDL), reflecting the addition of distance learning to the center's programs. From 2000 to 2009, adult outreach boomed with the number of matriculated students increasing from less than 98 to approximately 600 with a commensurate increase in gross revenues, locations, and staffing.

The 2009 Self-Study for Middle States devoted an entire chapter to the CCEDL recommending:

> The Dean of CCEDL, in consultation with the Provost/Senior Vice President and the President of the College, should investigate the possibility of expanding the role of the Center to provide graduate offerings to nontraditional students.
> (Elizabethtown College Self-Study Committee, 2009, p. 97)

> The CCEDL should develop its internet-based resources and delivery of courses, and should consider the viability of offering an option to complete some degrees or certificate programs exclusively through distance learning.
> (Elizabethtown College Self-Study Committee, 2009, p. 97)

Middle States' (MSCHE), in its decision to reaccredit EC in 2009, identified as a source of institutional pride:

> (the) rapid growth of the Center for Continuing Education and Distance Learning (CCEDL) with a delivery model characterized by rigorous standards for curriculum and instruction based on well-articulated learning outcomes.
> (Accreditation Visiting Team, 2009, p. 4)

The report by Middle States' also commended the CCEDL:

> The CCEDL is commended for its rigorous approach to the assessment of student learning outcomes and to the evaluation of instruction, both utilized for continuous improvement of the programs offered.
> (Accreditation Visiting Team, 2009, p. 21)

It also suggested:

> The CCEDL not only extends the College's mission to a regional adult audience but also generates revenues important to the sustainability of the College over time.
> (Accreditation Visiting Team, 2009, p. 22)

Observations/Analysis

The two reports, ten years apart, could not have been more different. The 1999 self-study showed little understanding of the reasons for the decline in adult learner enrollments and little understanding of the adult learner herself. Rather than utilize and integrate the real needs of the adult student to guide any and all attempts at solving CE's problems, this self-study relied, rather, on the needs and perspectives of the traditional academic departments and full-time faculty. These declarations by the self-study assured their irrelevancy.

Yet, by 2009, something had changed in EC's response to the needs of the adult student market. This change produced CE behavior that reinvigorated CE enrollment and CE financial contributions to the college. (This latter rose from a negative percentage of EC's total revenue, to approximately 10% of EC's total revenue).

The writers of the 1999 self-study operated strongly from the political frame; for them, the restorative power for CE rolled solidly down the traditional pathway of full-time curricula and full-time faculty.

There were some CE breakthroughs under the 1999 self-study driven by critical theory's impact on the whole system at EC. Still, the 1999 writers abandoned the creation and structure of the CCE; their vision saw adult learning at EC as an extension of the traditional program. They opted to defend the status quo and the reigning hegemony, burying the CCE under a mountain of bureaucratic rationality.

Takeaways

- Strive for representation among the producers of such reports as those discussed above.
- Make sure your perspective is heard and acknowledged; this must include the perspective of the 38-year-old working adult student. Let her voice be heard.
- Resign yourself to patience and persistence in countering the perspectives of the status quo (articulated by administrators, full-time faculty, full-time students, etc.).

42 *Accreditation and Continuing Education*

- Know the politics driving the report producers. Where's the power? Who are the decision-makers? How do they decide? What have they decided?
- Self-identify as an outspoken advocate for critical theory and its positive impacts on the organization.
- As such an advocate, seek out allies rather than friends.

These takeaways may seem targeted on start-up programs but they need not be; they are effective for existing programs or as evaluative guidelines for programs that exist and are being evaluated. They are designed to be flexible in their application.

7 New Plan for Continuing Education – Part I

The college hired me in early 2000 as dean of the recently renamed Center for Community Education (CCE), now referred to as the Center for Continuing Education and Distance Learning (CCEDL). I was the first dean of the center since the 1980's. I replaced a director. This upgrade was a sign of EC's intent to revitalize adult learning. I also came with a relatively fresh doctorate in philosophy-history (although I earned the Ph.D. when I turned 50). In general, hiring a dean with a doctorate in a traditional academic subject was designed to smooth my way into the ranks of traditional faculty. Not a bad strategy.

In discussions prior to my hire in February 2000, administrators, faculty, staff, students, and alumni struck a common chord – I would be expected to increase the number of matriculated students, thereby increasing gross revenues; I also was expected to keep costs as low as possible, thereby increasing net revenues to the college. Some of these groups did not speak in an open manner about these goals but rather spoke in terms of increasing diversity on campus. Yet the chief goals were clearly financial, judged by the responses I received to my questions.

I undertook a four-month study of the past, the present and the future of EC's adult outreach. The product was a document that used a marketing framework to understand what had happened – in short, the self-study recommendations of 1999 perpetuated a massive marketing failure that resulted in EC offerings that were irrelevant or inaccessible to its regional adult learning market. This failure doomed EC's adult outreach and suppressed adult learning; especially during the years when competition was increasing and was succeeding in meeting the needs of individual market members. CCEDL started out with 98 adult learners in degree-completion programs in 2000. A competitor in 2000 claimed, reliably, 800 adult learners.

The study resulted in a new Continuing Education Plan (CEP 2000) that not only addressed this market failure, not only reaffirmed the original basis of the CCE of 1972, but also, quite intentionally, relied on the application of critical theory across the board to challenge the way things were done. From structures of accountability to the identification of and use of affiliated faculty, to truly accelerated courses (5- or 8-week sessions with reduced contact hours, 20 or 30 per session) critical theory informed CEP 2000 and reconfigured the power and politics behind it.

In particular, CEP 2000 rejected the traditional centers of power, politics, and legitimacy – the matrix within which the CCEDL operated – the learning community. The 1999 self-study desired these centers to remain untouched by any change:

> This plan (CEP) must effectively integrate CE programs with the mainstream academic programs and must have the support and involvement of full-time faculty and departments.
> (Elizabethtown College Self-Study Committee, 1999, p. 29)

CEP 2000's analysis sought and found other centers which could create new pathways over which power, politics, and legitimacy could roll; for example, 1972's creation of the CCE was such a center, especially for legitimacy, and allowed the CEP 2000 of April 2000 to be cast, not only as a plan to revitalize but as a plan to reaffirm past practice; so the plan was both forward looking (innovative) and backward looking (traditional). A new breed of faculty was another such center – labeled affiliated faculty whose employment status was part-time; they were facilitator-practitioners, as opposed to teacher-scholars, who brought practical insights to the classroom and played an important role in the CCEDL's governance and restructuring of the academic departments to be more loose and more democratic. Additionally, another new center and its pathway of governance for the CCEDL was the Council for Academic Management (CAM); it oversaw both academic and administrative governance. CAM membership included administrators, CCEDL faculty, current students, alumni, and community representatives. By design, full-time faculty and traditional administrators were excluded. However, at any one time, the president and/or provost senior vice president sat on the Council. The CCEDL Dean sat as permanent chair. CAM was a small body ranging from between eight and 15 members over its lifetime and it supported qualities that were highly valued by the CCEDL – such as agility and flexibility and the eight transformative tasks of critical learning theory. The CAM functioned as advisory to the CCEDL dean. By 2015, lead facilitators sat on the Council. Remember that sooner or later, CE affiliated faculty will start behaving like traditional faculty. At one point the CAM tried to move faculty compensation to the agenda. That discussion never happened.

Accountability appeared to be spread throughout the CCEDL: lead facilitators, CAM membership, and various task forces. But all roads of accountability and responsibility led to the CCEDL dean. The dean was the highly visible point of accountability and responsibility. In short, the dean was accountable and responsible for the academic and financial performance of the center. The dean reported to the provost/senior vice president and was a member of the president's senior staff. This clarity of accountability and senior staff membership were invaluable in the dean's ability to perform quickly, flexibly, and to move the CCEDL ahead.

The plan for revitalizing and reaffirming Continuing Education at EC in 2000 was a radical departure from the way stakeholders had learned to think about higher education. The plan had the nervous support of the president. (He gave just enough support for the plan to succeed and with success his support increased). And the skeptical support of the provost/dean of faculty. (He delicately walked a tight rope between constituencies some of which were very hostile to the plan.) The plan was vetted with infrastructure groups whose support would be essential for its success. (IT, records and registration, financial aid, etc.) I went before the traditional College's Faculty Assembly with the plan, not asking for approval but for informational purposes only. There seemed to be little interest from the full-time faculty. There were only two questions proffered. Many faculty and administrators stood on the sideline, waiting to see which way things would break. (This group in waiting would become a more or less permanent part of the landscape through which the CCEDL wandered. Unless the group was immediately necessary for the CCEDL to move on, the wait and see group served several useful purposes and could, quite frankly, be practically ignored). CCEDL staff, breaking the tradition of seemingly endless collegiality, moved rapidly in advancing the plan; the CAM approved it and from there it went to the Academic Affairs Committee of the Board (AAC), then it moved to the full Board of Trustees (BOT) All trustee bodies approved the plan which was structured around three possible scenarios – from conservative to liberal. These scenarios strongly linked certain new or strengthened CCEDL structures and characteristics to CCEDL performance; the plan was filled with *if* ... *then* ... statements. The plan defined each scenario's outcomes in financial terms.

Meanwhile, a group of faculty from the business department wrote a letter to the provost/dean of faculty bemoaning the CEP which, in their judgment, would flood the college with unqualified students; these students would irreparably damage the status and prestige of the college. The provost/dean of faculty wisely heard them out while pointing out that nothing was in place yet and that there was nothing to evaluate yet. With this letter, a debate over CEP 2000 broke the surface. The environment in which this debate took place was one of increasing hostility between the CCEDL and the Business Department. Members of the department and members of CCEDL tried to improve this environment. However, it did reach the point of personal threats against staff.

In April 2000, undeterred and with trustee approval in its pocket, CCEDL forged ahead with scheduling, staffing, preparation of learning modules, and new accelerated courses targeted to commence in fall (September 2000).

Observations/Analysis

It was risky to design a CEP that proposed centers and pathways of power, politics, and legitimacy that were so different from those mandated in the self-study of 1999. It took a concerted effort by the CCEDL team to surmount this hurdle. The implementation of critical theory so threatened the status quo that enemies seemed to appear from beneath every rock turned. But the risk had to be taken if the goals (both financial and academic) of the plan were to be achieved. The CEP 2000 managed to link higher financial performance to the new centers in a convincing way.

The CEP 2000's acceptance would not have been possible without the measured support of the president and the provost/dean of faculty. Such support needed to be given carefully and gracefully so that other stakeholder groups would not be absolutely alienated.

Positioning the requested trustee vote on the CEP 2000 as a reaffirmation of the legitimacy of the CCE of 1972 was a very strong point in its favor. It certainly did not guarantee approval, but made approval much more likely, by taking the sharp edges off the real innovations contained in the plan.

To understand the events of the day, the political frame is most useful. Again, the rhetoric of the debate was that of academic quality, but behind this rhetoric were political questions of who controls learning at EC? Would the politics of the day allow for a competing model to run alongside the traditional model? At heart it was about power and who wielded the politics it generated. So too, the symbolic frame is a close second in explanatory power – what would CEP 2000's implementation symbolize for the college? What meaning would it send to those beyond the walls of the college? Could it symbolize the status and prestige supportive of high rankings? Did that matter?

The CEP 2000 was enlivened by the tasks of critical theory and in this harkened back to the 1972 CCE. A review of the verbs associated with those tasks, reinforces this fact. The CE 2000 plan:

- *Challenged*
- *Contested*
- *Unmasked*

- *Overcame*
- *Liberated*
- *Reclaimed*
- *Democratized*

These tasks threatened the status quo and the familiar pathways of power which carried the end product to its final users.

Takeaways

If you undertake a plan to revitalize, reaffirm, or change your institution's adult learning:

- Be bold and let critical theory enliven your plan. It's one way that your plan will succeed. Boldness will bolster confidence which will go a long way to assuring success.
- Look back historically and find similar programs or pieces of programs your institution undertook. You will be surprised at what you will find and thankful for its utility in moving ahead.
- Cultivate support for your plan at the highest levels: trustees, president, provost; it need not be 100% and enthusiastic, you only need the level necessary to advance your plan.
- Realize that the effects of what you are proposing threaten institutionalized stakeholders and that they will resist any change.
- Give top decision-makers options in the form of different scenarios. Link various versions of the plan to various levels of performance. This can be very effective in carrying the day.
- Prominently highlight how the plan will generate increased gross and net revenues. Keep these projections enticing but realistic. Find the sweet spot.
- Keep the plan as simple as possible – opt for fewer pages and fewer steps toward the plan's goals.
- Although accountability may be democratically dispersed throughout your organization, counter this with a highly visible point of final accountability; someone who takes final responsibility for all things. This will make your proposal more credible and result in a smoother running organization.
- Be intentional in your use of critical theory to garnish your adult learning community.

Part Three
Faculty

If we teach today's students as we taught yesterday's we rob them of tomorrow.
John Dewey

8 New Plan for Continuing Education – Part II

The Center for Community Education (CCE) in 1972 and the Center for Continuing Education and Distance Learning (CCEDL) in 2000 supported the development of a new type of hybrid faculty that was steeped in the values of critical theory. These hybrids could go by any number of names – Adjunct Faculty or Contingent Faculty (a statement of employment status with the college), New Faculty Majority (advocacy group based on employment status with CE), Affiliated Faculty (part-time employment status with CE to facilitate accelerated courses plus unbundled tasks such as learning model revision, writing new learning modules, governance service, lead facilitators, etc. paid by fee). The latter might be known as the facilitator/practitioner model as opposed to the teacher/scholar model common to full-time faculty. We chose affiliated faculty mainly because of the depth attributable to the importance of the unbundled tasks which the name captured. We had a pool of approximately two hundred affiliated faculty members in total. Active affiliated faculty (those teaching in six or more sessions per academic year) numbered approximately 90.

Affiliated faculty's employment status was part-time and their base pay was based on classroom facilitation only. This is to say that many of the tasks associated with faculty were bundled and compensated by fee when unbundled and successfully completed – tasks such as learning module development, learning module revision, mentoring new faculty.

We might call the governance task group one of the most important of these unbundled tasks. These were very important to the CCEDL and one of the salient distinguishing markers of faculty that was affiliated rather than adjunct or contingent. These governance tasks included things such as serving as lead facilitators, oversight of learning module development and maintenance, curriculum creation/revision, service on the Council on Academic Management (CAM), and the assessment of potential new faculty. These facilitator-practitioners brought the real world into the CCEDL classroom and served as the central pool of intellectual capital for the CCEDL. Their competence as affiliated faculty was determined by a special assessment process; this process had a very low pass rate of about 30%. The process was designed to measure and assess content mastery as well as the ability to relate to and implement methodologies that honored the learning characteristics of adults. (See next chapter for a more detailed account of this faculty assessment process including the growing impact of internet-based learning.) This stood opposed to measurement of competence by simple previous employment and recommendation alone as is usually done when academic departments hire more traditional adjuncts. Expectations of affiliated faculty were high. Management expected affiliated faculty to attend at least two faculty developments per year as well as two faculty dinners per year. Raises in compensation were associated with attendance at these events, the number of unbundled tasks (especially governance tasks) undertaken and completed, and the number of courses facilitated.

Management of and support of affiliated faculty was in the purview of the CCEDL associate dean.

In the beginning, the CCEDL borrowed curricula and courses from the traditional Elizabethtown College (EC) programs. These were revised to fit an accelerated (5-week and 8-week) academic session and syllabi were transformed into learning modules based on course, major, and program student learning outcomes which were measurable. Lead facilitators (similar to department heads) oversaw this curricular task to carefully monitor and keep the curricula fresh. These curricular tasks included:

- Working with facilitating faculty.
- Discipline activities.
- Special taskforces.
- Pulling dated learning modules.
- Translating on campus courses to hybrid (online/on campus mix) or completely internet-based courses. (This became a major task; by 2015, 67% of courses offered by the CCEDL were completely internet-based; the faculty assessment was adjusted to measure abilities in the virtual classroom; and this continued to grow as a part of the faculty assessment process.)

Significantly, all learning modules were work done for hire and were the property of EC and the CCEDL. This was a clear-cut approach to certain intellectual property rights. This approach appeared in every affiliated faculty facilitation contract issued. This provided an appreciated clarity when intellectual property issues might arise.

Observations/Analysis

The development of a new CE faculty model – affiliated faculty – allowed the CCEDL to exhibit that its faculty was a center of power, politics, critical theory, and legitimacy. The structural frame helps to explain how the CCEDL structures, such as its affiliated faculty, were important in building a nimble, responsive learning organization that could move at dizzying speed when compared to more traditional structures. Political questions arose from the full-time traditional faculty; the language of these questions had a strong symbolic component.

There was no central location where affiliated faculty congregated regularly (CCEDL had six locations). As facilitator-practitioners, the affiliated faculty was scattered throughout the region. This made providing opportunities for them to get together, regularly, very important – thus the faculty dinners, faculty developments, faculty socials, and so forth.

CCEDL's affiliated faculty often served as an example of how the full-time faculty might be improved; especially on the question of how to integrate faculty whose employment status was part-time into meaningful governance activities. This was an important contribution of elements of critical theory to the more traditional structures and perspectives.

CCEDL affiliated faculty are conduits of and implementers of critical theory and its associated tasks. This plays out on the side of things that may not be as clear as they could be; to clarify involves how affiliated faculty are identified and hired and will be dealt with in the next chapter.

Thus, new avenues of access, including the Internet, were encouraged through which new stakeholders had the opportunity to feed their experiences to enrich CE programs.

Takeaways

- Spend the time and resources to do those things necessary to produce cohesion and comprehensiveness among the affiliated faculty: things like formal developments and less formal social events like faculty dinners or socials. Remember affiliated faculty may be spread out widely throughout the region and they are hungry for belonging to something cohesive.
- Implement a Facilitator of the Year program to celebrate these new forms of faculty as well as the individuals who excel at implementing them.
- Implement a comprehensive control system for learning modules. Do this as soon as you can to avoid loss of control over your learning modules which is always a danger.

54 Faculty

- Review learning modules (new and revised) and get sign off from learning module author, lead facilitators, director (or assistant/associate dean) of faculty and curriculum, or dean of CCEDL. Many eyes improve the final product.
- Do periodic reviews to make sure learning modules are being facilitated rather than content just being taught.
- Make sure end-of-course student evaluations contain a robust section that allows student evaluation of faculty.
- *Note: Sooner or later, your affiliated faculty will begin acting like full-time faculty.* Have strategies you can fall back on to counter this recidivism – especially on intellectual property rights and fidelity to following learning module standards.
- Position the behavior of affiliated faculty as the keystone of your academic quality control efforts.

9 New Plan for Continuing Education – Part III

Based on its financial and academic success, the Center for Continuing Education and Distance Learning (CCEDL) became the School of Continuing and Professional Studies (SCPS) in 2010. This name better communicated the autonomous and unique nature of the unit; still united at the highest levels such as mission, the SCPS remained a unit of Elizabethtown College (EC).

Affiliated faculty remained the major strength of the SCPS based on their effectiveness in the classroom with adults. And it remains the chief way the values of critical theory, its power and its politics become operational throughout the program. How did the SCPS reach this level of achievement? How did the school achieve it consistently? How did faculty facilitate a course rather than just teach it? How did the SCPS choose those faculty most likely to succeed?

The SCPS relied heavily on what it termed the faculty assessment process for these successes. Two versions were simultaneously developed an on campus version and an online version. The skills required for success in each venue differ significantly.

The school announces a general call for those with needed content expertise; this is usually done through the regional newspapers. Credentials are submitted to the School – a master's degree is required and a resume. The school looked for experience that indicated the candidate would succeed in the adult classroom – a combination of previous facilitation with a graduate degree, for example. No fewer than three SCPS staff members initially screened submissions, distilling them to a number of candidates somewhere between ten and 25. The SCPS invited these candidates to participate in its faculty assessment process.

Assessors (those who actually assess faculty candidates) were selected from the various stakeholder groups – SCPS administrators, current SCPS students, alumni, SCPS faculty, Council of Academic Management (CAM) members, etc. This gave a voice to many groups who had none previously. Practicing democracy in faculty selection, if you will.

The faculty assessment is held on a Saturday. Faculty candidates start at 9:00 a.m. and end at 1:00 p.m. Assessors start at 8:00 a.m. and finish when all candidates have been assessed, usually sometime after 4:00 p.m. Faculty candidates perform a list of activities on which they are assessed. These activities include:

- Submit an essay on the facilitation of adult learners in your discipline.
- Submit a current resume.
- Evaluate a student-written essay with detailed feedback.
- Submit to a personal interview.
- Give a class presentation (includes students).
- Participate in a leaderless group activity (how do you achieve consensus among widely differing viewpoints)?

Candidates are broken into groups so that each candidate will be assessed by at least three different assessors. After candidates leave, assessors evaluate candidates' performance by colored dots: red (no), yellow (caution), green (yes). Strict rubrics, reflecting the current mix of power, politics, and critical theory are used for evaluating each activity's performance; these rubrics are used consistently by the assessors. There is a numerical score that each candidate achieves for each part of the rubric. Total numerical scores are equated to the colors mentioned above. Final performance of the candidates as a group and as individuals is recorded on a large chart using the large colored dots. What presents, then, is a colorful, highly visual representation of the candidates' performance. When all the candidates have been assessed, they are dismissed.

There is then a discussion of candidates guided by the chart. Some are easy – all green (yes), all red (no). Most are a mix and need to be discussed fully. Some may be invited to join the affiliated faculty on the condition that they are mentored by more experienced facilitators. Assessors support or don't support certain candidates – this discussion is lively and is based on the rubric scores.

Observations/Analysis

Over 15 years of use at EC, the average pass rate for the faculty assessment is about 30%. The assessment is highly predictive of success in the adult classroom. Successful candidates must attend a new faculty orientation. They then join the SCPS affiliated faculty pool. From this pool, they may be offered facilitation assignments. Attendance at regular faculty developments is expected. A mentoring process is also available for those who feel the need for it. Five-week or eight-week sessions are the only session types that are compensated for. No affiliated faculty has a contract longer than this. The contract they are given reinforces that learning modules or, indeed, any learning materials developed for a course is work for hire and belongs to the college and that facilitators may be removed from a classroom for poor performance by the dean of the SCPS.

It should be noted that no claim is made here for the exclusivity of the faculty assessment process to EC. The process was developed during the period after the Second World War by the corporate sector. And indeed today many schools utilize it even if they do so with some significant modifications.

Because of the human resources involved, faculty assessments are very costly. The SCPS usually did two assessments per year. You want to make them as productive as possible.

Note: no one facilitates who has not passed the faculty assessment. (The faculty assessment process is one of SCPS' major quality control mechanisms.)

As the main intake for the school's intellectual capital, the human resource frame informs the school of the fit between affiliated faculty and the organization (system) and recognizes the reciprocal needs between all parties. The school provides support to its faculty to help ensure success and opportunities for growth.

The rubrics by which faculty candidates are evaluated are infused with the values of critical theory and andragogy – these values are captured by the verbs of the eight transformative tasks of critical theory. Rubrics are built upon these action words:

- Challenging ideology
- Contesting hegemony
- Unmasking power
- Overcoming alienation
- Learning liberation
- Reclaiming reason
- Practicing democracy
- Contesting bureaucratic rationality

A similar process builds a set of rubrics that convey the values of andragogy (Knowles, 1970). When scoring activities, these two sets of values intertwine and those faculty candidates who do well will stand out and be selected to join the SCPS affiliated faculty pool.

The assessment is an outstanding way to inject these values and tasks into your front-line personnel, your learning modules, and thereby, into your whole program. And, as symbolic leaders, these faculty members will have the opportunity to interpret critical theory and andragological values and tasks to enlighten specific classroom situations.

The political frame usually comes into play from those outside of the SCPS who can, understandably, be threatened by the process of faculty assessment. Traditional roadways to power, politics, learning theory and legitimacy are being bypassed and are being replaced by more democratic ones through more democratic protocols. This is a political problem and you need to be sensitive to opportunities for collaborations and consensus building that can defuse the situation.

Takeaways

- Do not neglect attention to and use of the faculty assessment. Make it a priority. And a cornerstone of your quality control system. Your adult learning programs can fail or succeed based on its use. Faculty assessments are time-consuming and expensive to run but they need to take place.
- Steadfastly support your affiliated faculty. This can range from providing handouts for class to taking the time to brainstorm about how to facilitate certain problematic content. This can be costly but must be done. All facilitators, at one time or another, have voiced to me their appreciation for this support and how it differentiates EC's adult learning programs from those at other institutions of higher education (IHEs).
- *Remember: no one facilitates who has not passed the faculty assessment.*
- Build in opportunities for affiliated faculty to get together – dinners, developments, socials, review taskforces, etc. These opportunities build group identity and loyalty. Include in some of these activities not only affiliated faculty but full-time traditional faculty, too. Both groups will benefit from the contact with each other.
- *Resign yourself to the fact that affiliated faculty will, sooner or later, start behaving like full-time traditional faculty and will need to be corrected.* Don't neglect or ignore this. Facilitation from a learning module is very structured. Faculty will give you pushback wanting to do it their way; you should be prepared with strategies to either bring these people back or to cut these people loose.
- Remember that through the faculty assessment process and the development and use of affiliated faculty, you are opening new avenues of access to new talent. This will threaten those who are unfamiliar with

this new model of faculty. Be aware that this will happen. Be approachable and answer questions cheerfully.
- Be very intentional about integrating the values of current power, politics, critical theory, and andragogy into faculty assessment rubrics whether on campus or online.

Part Four
Locations

10 New Plan for Continuing Education – Part IV

Elizabethtown College's (EC's) Continuing Education (CE) outreach operated from two locations as far back as the early 1950s. As of today, the School of Continuing and Professional Studies (SCPS) unit operates from six locations – four in Lancaster County (EC main campus in Elizabethtown, Pennsylvania; on the campus of Franklin and Marshall College in Lancaster; Harrisburg Area Community College [HACC] in Lancaster; Lancaster Intermediate Unit 13 (Lancaster IU13]) one in Harrisburg, Pennsylvania (Dixon University Center) and one in York, Pennsylvania (Saint Charles Way Corporate Center).

Why did the SCPS expand its locations in this fashion?

SCPS viewed additional locations as an engine of growth. As of 2015, this held true for every location; and it was true by any method of calculation. Each location made a positive contribution to SCPS' profitability. There are many ways to structure additional locations. SCPS – Elizabethtown: main campus, Harrisburg: academic consortium, York: free standing corporate center, Lancaster: main campus of Franklin and Marshall College, Lancaster: campus of HACC, Lancaster: County Intermediate Unit. It is important to take advantage of what is and how it could be changed into what ought to be. Some location structures are obvious in how they may best contribute; others may require some sculpting. Most structures can be made to fit in some positive way; although there are some that cannot.

SCPS students consistently inform us through surveying that they prefer to take their classes close to their place of employment and close to where they reside. These locations partially address this market desire. Each SCPS location is an appropriate mix of office space, classroom space, and technology (mostly classroom space).

Many argue that with the explosive growth of online learning, physical locations are obsolete. While online learning has grown rapidly (67% of SCPS' courses are offered over the internet) it doesn't necessarily follow that physical locations will shrivel up and fade away. A lot depends on who your online user is and where she is located. It's true that the internet allows a spectacular outreach that cannot be captured by a physical location; yet, most of SCPS' online users are local to the region and want personal contact with an advisor regularly. This may mean that locations should shrink to more of an office configuration and less of a classroom configuration. Location personnel in this latter configuration are more like life-counselors than academic advisors – providing a wide-ranging array of personal services; and most of all, standing ever more as a representative of the home institution.

Whatever the case, there's a lot of preparation and research that goes into identifying and selecting an additional location. Opening such a location can be risky and preparation helps mitigate this risk. Who else will you be sharing the location with? Does it matter? Why or why not?

Observations/Analysis

Growth is not guaranteed through the addition of locations, and significant risk may be associated with such additions. But experience teaches that they can also create new opportunities for growth. Sound research can help identify winners and losers.

Online growth may not do away with the need for locations, but may change what that location looks like, how it is configured, and how it is staffed.

Beware of overreach; by all means avoid thinking "if we build it, they will come". You'll have to work hard to get new students through a new location.

Unless circumstances are particularly unique, set the same standards for all locations; be scrupulous in adhering to them. This applies especially to the values of critical theory and andragogy. And this will be a concern of regional accreditors.

While strictly a structural concern, the addition of locations carries with it strong elements of the symbolic frame. Whatever the location looks like or whoever you have working there, to the student they are your college; so make sure they accurately reflect your home institution and its values.

Be aware that there is always pressure on locations to fly-away into their own realm of autonomy. Find effective ways to keep them meaningfully connected. Try rotating regular staff meetings among different locations. Make sure location personnel are included in your communication loops.

Takeaways

- Scrupulously develop separate financials for each location and when making comparisons make sure you are comparing apples to apples and oranges to oranges.

- Make sure you are clear-eyed when analyzing location financials. It's not a sin to cut or downgrade a location that is not performing up to expected standards.
- Choose locations wisely; do your preparation and research and make certain you consider power and its politics and their expressions at the new location.
- Remember that to students each location is a projection of your home institution. Make sure it's realistic and the best one possible.
- Staff wisely. Make sure that location directors understand your standards fully and are enthusiastic about implementing them. To this end, consider separate development activities for location staff and target those developments on the basic values that hold your programs together.

Part Five
Class Conflict

> The history of all hitherto existing society is the history of class struggles. Freeman and slave, patrician and plebian, lord and serf, guild-master and journeyman, in a word, oppressor and oppressed, stood in constant opposition to one another, carried on an uninterrupted, now hidden, now open fight, a fight that each time ended, either in a revolutionary reconstitution of society at large, or in the common ruin of the contending classes.
>
> The Communist Manifesto

11 Conflicts between Adult and Traditional Students

An issue of the student newspaper at Elizabethtown College (EC), the *Etownian*, was scathing in its assertion that allowing adult learners into a School of Continuing and Professional Studies (SCPS) MBA program, would significantly damage the prestige and status of the College, thereby devaluing, wholesale, an EC diploma for everyone. It was not really an argument that the *Etownian* set forth because it was notable for its lack of engageable content. At one level, the EC students who made the assertions, were merely siphoning off the poisonous atmosphere created by a venomous exchange between the SCPS and the Business Department about who should offer a new MBA program at the college and for which audience. Never rising to the level of argument, the editors simply asserted a general ad hominem attack on anyone who might be considered an adult learner. For being impressionable, the editors may be forgiven and be advised not to be so much so. Yet, there was something darker involved here. Something that sprang from deep psychological currents that fed off the *Us/Them* dichotomy. The assertions never rose to the level of identifying or perceiving adult students as true Others, corralled by true class boundaries that shattered, dangerously, when they collided with different class boundaries. As mere assertions, rather than the result of deeper thought they should have been answered immediately by either the provost/senior vice president or the president. But they were not. As dean of the SCPS, I submitted a written response taking issue with the weak assertions put forth by the newspaper.

A more nuanced, but essentially identical approach had appeared in a letter written by several business department faculty members immediately after implementation of the CEP 2000. The letter went to the president and the provost/dean of faculty and attempted to make the case that adult learners were merely "fannies in the seats" meant to generate revenue but they were academically unfit for academic programs at EC. Still there was little arguable content in this case.

At a meeting of the Student Senate, the supposed class conflict approach to EC's adult outreach again raised its head. The president of EC, who was in attendance, stated that the full-time students should be thankful for the adult learners whose tuition subsidized their full-time tuition rate. Despite the noblest of intentions, the president's statement was another approach to these adult learners that treated them like a separate class, this time, flush with cash.

More seriously and as proffered in the introduction, how revenues generated by adult learner enrollment are recorded in the college budget can reinforce the notion of these learners as true second class students.

Conversations, even informal ones, reinforce this stereotype. Often, EC students are referred to as "the kids". This is usually due to thoughtlessness on the speaker's part. But for whatever reason, the term would strike the 38-year old, single mother as odd and perhaps even degrading.

Observations/Analysis

Classes of students will inevitably form and clash according to Friedrich Engels and Karl Marx as stated in the *Communist Manifesto* (1848). This clash becomes the engine of change, moving things along from past, present, and into the future. The clash itself provides the traction to move into the future. In the present case, EC's adult learner outreach created a self-conscious group of learners who challenged the premises, beliefs, and visions of the dominant student class from the position of possessing different interests, goals, and perspectives. The language of first class (or primary class) and second class (or secondary class) can be hurtful. But even if hurtful the conflict itself could be productive – especially by injecting positive aspects of critical theory into the organization. Class conflict, at this organizational level could: challenge ideology, contest hegemony, unmask power, overcome alienation, liberate learning, reclaim reason, practice democracy, and contest bureaucratic rationality.

Paradoxically, those servicing adult learners through a reliance on the premises of andragogy, themselves draw boundaries around these learners that look a lot like class boundaries. Overemphasis on differences in learning styles can foster this. It is again a case where class conflict can produce positive outcomes as well as negative ones.

The political frame may be very active in cases of class conflict especially concerning the distribution of resources; this aspect emphasizes conflict over power. So too the symbolic frame reveals what the different class identities mean to the participants.

Takeaways

- Adult learner outreach will produce a self-aware class of adult learners with interests that conflict with those of traditional students; this conflict is usually political and usually deals with the distribution and allocation of resources. An emphasis on class creation and the conflict it creates can be hurtful and degrading, but it can also be positive and uplifting as well.
- Try to harness class formation and conflict and turn it into something productive. Class conflict can be another way to inject elements of critical theory into the organization/system.
- The development of student classes has its origins in more than one political interest group. It can be very important to know which group is operational in any particular case.

Part Six
Staff

12 Stresses and Strains of Critical Theory on the Front Line

In the integration of power, politics, and critical theory (CT) within the School of Continuing and Professional Studies' (SCPS') adult learning programs, administrative staff come in second only to affiliated faculty. This administrative staff totaled three in February 2000; by July 2015, it totaled seventeen. Over the decade and a half, three were asked to leave and one left on their own initiative. This administrative face of SCPS' adult learning programs included:

- **Academic Advisors:** professional advisors who stand in opposition to the faculty/advisors of the traditional program. They are distributed by location. These advisors handle a great deal of registrar-like functions for the adult learners. They are, importantly, advocates for the adult learners in their interpretation and application of academic and administrative rules and regulations.
- **Academic Advisor Data Base Support Specialist:** provide hard data support that was needed by advising staff with regard to decision-making. Must be creative in working with differing systems to produce usable data.
- **Associate Dean:** recruits appropriate faculty and provides support for them as needed. This support is not only material but also includes a collegial dimension to build cohesion among an otherwise widely dispersed group.
- **Dean of Enrollment Services:** responsible for setting and achieving adult learning enrollment goals as well as coordinating with financial aid.
- **Admissions Coordinators:** implement enrollment plans, strategy, and tactics. These coordinators are the first faces the prospective adult learner sees when they make contact with the SCPS. Very important relationship positions.

- **Dean of Student Services:** serves as liaison with other Elizabethtown College (EC) support offices such as Records and Registration, Financial Aid, Special Needs, etc. Oversees academic advising function. Strong function of advocating for adult learners' interests.
- **Director of Curriculum:** responsible for course scheduling; (this is a very challenging function and must be done with care) and strategies and tactics to keep curricula fresh and current as well as how to introduce new courses and curricula. Works with advisory groups from, business, health care, and community.
- **Office Manager:** coordinates and supports SCPS office operations as well as affiliated faculty support. This position easily falls victim to stressful overwork. Highly visible as the source of almost all office and program support.
- **Location Managers:** carry out program standards at remote locations with integrity. This position is subject to divided loyalties. And tension can develop between the central unit and the location.
- **SCPS Dean:** advocates for adult learning programs and their support for the president's senior staff. Accountable for the appropriate functioning and advancement of the school. Final link in the chain of accountability. Works with other senior staff to promote interests of adult learning programs.
- **Non-Credit Coordinator:** oversees all non-credit programs – Japanese Summer Language Program, Learning in Retirement, Professional Development, etc. Care should be taken that these non-credit programs do not bleed too many resources from revenue producing (credit) programs. Some non-credit programs, however, can be very profitable.

In general, the staff of the SCPS experienced all the issues of the larger institution writ small. They served as the face of the college to adult learners and reflected the current state of power, politics, and critical theory back to the adult learners.

Especially important in this respect were the academic advisors who became personal conduits of what the school was all about. Relationship management was very important in making this connection. How appropriate academic rules and regulations were identified and applied in any single case proclaimed a great deal about the vibrancy of critical theory. And spoke a great deal about the true power pathways of the institution.

The SCPS administrative staff positions contain a special dimension – and that is the dimension of high stress. This stress comes from sheer numbers. One of the goals of the SCPS is to keep costs as low as possible to improve the net. One result, unfortunately, was a workload or caseload that was intimidating. All employment positions involve some level of stress, but the stress found in positions serving adult learning is especially acute.

Similar to the faculty assessment rubric, potential administrative staff should be evaluated against their own rubric that is designed to measure critical theory values in specific cases as well as how well the employee-candidate deals with high stress levels. This is a bit more complicated than with faculty, since many of these interpretations involved personnel from other offices whose approaches to rules and regulations did not encompass the values the SCPS sought.

To the eight transformative tasks, advocacy of the adult learner interests must be added. Flexibility and patience as well, plus an awareness of the circumstances adult learners find themselves in when returning to school. The hiring rubric should also measure the ability to work together as a team.

SCPS administrative staff did not deal with billing, financial aid, or special needs directly. Rather, SCPS administrative staff served as liaisons with those offices which served the entire college. Often, this resulted in conflict between the office and the SCPS. One important issue was transfer credit evaluation. This was an important task that should reside with the school and not the Records and Registration (RR) office. That office resisted handing over responsibility to SCPS vigorously. Different interests and standards could be honored by the school in a way the RR Office was unwilling to do. SCPS' motivation was to accept as many credits as possible in transfers within the boundaries of sound academic practice. This, of course, saved the adult learner money by not having to retake courses already taken. The RR office used much more universal and rigid standards – for example, in aging transfer credits more strictly and more strictly defining acceptable accrediting agencies. Much of SCPS' staff time was taken up in finding ways, when applying these standards, to soften their impact on the adult learner. Most times a way was found to do this to the benefit of the adult learner.

Observations/Analysis

As previously stated, administrative staff is second only to affiliated faculty as conduits of power, politics, and critical theory directly to the adult learner. From initial inquiry to program completion, opportunities abound to impact the adult learner with the new paths of power, their attendant politics, and the tasks of critical theory.

Rubrics measuring the attendant values need to be put into play when hiring administrative staff. These rubrics will differ from those used to select affiliated faculty but will contain similar values.

Academic advisors and admissions coordinators are an important part of your frontline interface with adult learners. It is especially important to fully support both.

Since your staff and the staff of the wider infrastructure will often be at odds over identification, implementation, and application of rules and regulations, a hostile relationship can develop between the two. This can be productive in sharpening your staffs' identity and place within the college. But be careful that this is not overdone so that it cannot be undone when necessary. You should look for opportunities to dampen the hostilities that are unnecessary.

It is not unusual for staff members to develop a following among adult students. Care must be taken that this does not become unreasonable attachment. Relationships can be intense in the process of recruiting and supporting the adult learner on her journey.

Sooner or later your administrative staff will start behaving like higher education bureaucrats.

Takeaways

- Take the time to develop a workable hiring rubric. Make sure that all staff are familiar with it and implement it.
- Encourage cross-training of positions; avoid isolated silos.
- As with affiliated faculty, provide the support staff require to do their jobs.
- Manage the relations between your staff and that of the wider college; hostility is to be expected but keep it under control; it can be used to sharpen your own offices' identities; find opportunities to bridge the hostilities.
- Have strategies prepared to defeat the tendency of staff to become higher education bureaucrats. Think about how to counter this tendency.
- If you have locations, rotate staff meetings among them to strengthen their ties to the adult learning programs you are growing.
- Design development opportunities; at least one a year. Make these opportunities rich in the type of experiences that will be relevant and appropriate.
- Set aside sufficient time to acknowledge and celebrate the quality of services delivered by this group.

Part Seven

The Rhetoric of Academic Quality

> Mighty Caesar! Dost thou lie so low?
> Are all thy conquests, glories, triumphs, spoils,
> Shrunk to this little measure?
> > Shakespeare, *Julius Caesar,* III.i.148

13 Faculty Assessment Process as a Gateway for Affiliated Faculty

Each of the eight transformative tasks by which critical theory operationalizes itself involve, in some fashion, the stripping away of facades to reveal the realities behind them. These main tasks of critical theory are reflected in the verbs associated with the eight transformative tasks:

- Challenging ideology
- Contesting hegemony
- Unmasking power
- Overcoming alienation
- Learning liberation
- Reclaiming reason
- Practicing democracy
- Contesting bureaucratic rationality

This unmasking function, related most closely to number three above, most often reveals true power pathways and the politics that support them. We have seen how discussions of the academic quality of adult learning programs were often used to mask these powerful realities.

Not meant to elicit substantial, real answers, about how things work, these rhetorical academic quality questions include ones like:

- Are there clear, appropriate learning outcomes at the class, course, and program levels?
- Is the achievement of these learning outcomes assessed? How? What level of confidence do you have in the assessment process?
- Are students adequately prepared for college-level academics? How do we know?
- Does accelerated learning work academically? What are its limits?

These questions serve a useful purpose, but not at the highest level and, more often than not, obfuscate real discussion and argument about power and its politics. Critical theory hammers the rhetorical facades these questions erect, revealing the truly salient questions about how power and politics are configured and operate in adult learning programs.

These salient questions include ones like:

- Who owns learning? Who and where are the decision-makers?
- Who owns the curriculum? With whom and where does this power reside?
- What power and political protocols govern the flow of power and decision-making?
- Who owns academic courses? What protocols build them into curricula and programs?
- What rights and privileges cluster around the exercise of academic power?
- What role do faculty and students play in setting educational goals and the pathways to them?

The rhetoric of academic quality would lead to actions like those undertaken by the student newspaper, letters by faculty, and actions by the president of the college. These were the easier questions to ask and answer and perhaps, in their answers, the most contentious ones. They were not unimportant questions and answers, just not the most important ones.

Observations/Analysis

Still, the rhetoric of academic quality serves an important institutional purpose. Its vocabulary forms a type of jail cell within which adult learning programs can be contained and imprisoned; it is a clever if deceptive usage, wielded by those who possess real, make-a-difference power; those who support ideology and hegemony, who mask power and support alienation, who suppress the liberation of learning, who reject the reclamation of reason, who stifle the practice of democracy, and who support the growth of bureaucratic rationality. Its language and vocabulary lay a pathway that only rarely advances towards the truth about power.

The rhetoric of academic quality effectively shields the status quo from dissembling attacks.

Takeaways

- Increase your awareness that oftentimes discussions and arguments about adult learning will be rhetorical and will generate a great deal of

heat but little light. Most of these discussions will revolve around the rhetorical language of academic quality.
- Be patient in these exchanges and take away what might be of value, but don't forget the important questions that are being avoided. Know what you are really talking about.
- Seek and find ways to address the rhetorical language of academic quality. Address what you can in a collegial way but don't give up too much. Use what look like familiar markers to signify quality even if they mean very different things on the adult learning landscape.
- Recognize that you are dealing with champions of the status quo; those who have a strong vested interest in thwarting change. Do not underestimate their power and persistence.
- Develop your own measures of success that are effective in interpreting the success of your adult learning programs.
- Growth in enrollment and revenues will be your strongest arguments for success.

Conclusion

We've used the experience of Elizabethtown College (EC) in south-central Pennsylvania with its adult outreach to suggest answers to questions about the vigorous growth of adult learning there: what happened at this small, independent college that made this growth possible? How did power, politics, and critical theory encourage or suppress adult learning? Do the answers to these questions tell us anything important about adult learning? Certainly, our analysis tells us that power, its political expressions, and the way it allocates resources and critical theory in its impacts on the structures of the adult learning community, are key elements in the encouraged growth or encouraged suppression of adult learning. How these elements are configured in relation to each other and in relation to elements outside the adult learning community is very important. Such elements and their various configurations can help us to understand how higher education operates in general.

The experience of EC in this regard from the early 1950s but in particular from 2000 to 2015, has been sifted down to seven topics subjected to organizational and analytical tools like those found in Bolman and Deal (2013) and in Brookfield (2005). It's helpful to envision these seven topics and their content as snapshots rather than anything more dynamic – frozen snippets in time, rather than more dynamic continua. My emphasis has been on the systemic impacts on the organization as opposed to on anything lesser. In general, the political frame/leadership and the symbolic frame/leadership are most useful in explaining the way things are. There are exceptions – Part Three: Faculty – for example, relies on the human resources frame/leadership in a way other topics do not; and a lot of that reliance rests on the notion that there is such a thing as proper fit between the individual and the adult learning organization.

Critical theory organizes, analyzes, and animates the spirit driving eight transformative tasks to completion:

- *Challenging ideology* that permeates the environment within which the individual student is called to learn in order to reveal hidden oppression

and inequity. Provides a new pair of lenses through which to discern the injustices of the status quo.
- *Contesting hegemony* to foster rejection of an unjust social order.
- *Unmasking power* to raise awareness of the roles various types of power play in our lives and how it is used and abused. A key element to succeeding in this task is to know how to identify the power that is real and effective.
- *Overcoming alienation* to claim freedom from manipulation.
- *Learning liberation* from the dominant ideology.
- *Reclaiming reason* to broaden its usage in all aspects of life. This fosters a deep-seated optimism in the way things turn out.
- *Practicing democracy* and learning to live with its contradictions. Promotes disorder rather than order and chaos rather than order.

And to these seven tasks, I add an eighth because of its growing ubiquity:

- *Contesting bureaucratic rationality* which promotes a dull and erroneous form of equality between all things (Merriam et al., 2007, p. 257).

These tasks challenge the adult learner, the system (organization), its administrators, and its faculty. And the tasks' impacts on organization are much more difficult to identify than the clearer-cut frames found in Bolman and Deal (2013). There is a general ignorance of critical theory's potential for examining practices or illuminating the nature of adult learning (Merriam et al., 2007, p. 253). This book hopes to substitute a basic level of awareness for this ignorance. Still, Bolman and Deal's (2013) frames can sharply enlighten the adult learning landscape while critical theory's contributions often generate more of a smoky murkiness that can obscure the lay of the land. It takes persistence and patience to analyze the impact of critical theory because of this characteristic.

Still, it would be short-sighted to view Bolman and Deal (2013) and Brookfield (2005) as only analytical tools. A good deal of their value lies in this functionality, but not all of it. Each possesses an element of agency, as we saw in the direct impacts critical theory has on the affiliated faculty and administrative staff hiring rubrics by which values were injected into hiring protocols.

There is a good deal of give and take between analytical tool and agency. By stressing analytical tool functioning, I have tried to provide the reader with perspectives and attitudes that are applicable to a wide range of institutions of higher education with the hope that this application will be fruitful. To add, directly, institutions for comparison and contrast with the EC experience, is beyond the scope of the present work. To do so runs the risk of losing a sharp focus that is necessary to understand difficult concepts like critical theory and how it serves to destroy facades to reveal the real power and its politics at work.

EC's adult outreach from the early 1950s to the 1980s might be characterized as an era of good feeling among a handful of local institutions. Status and prestige had yet to play their driving roles in establishing competitive rankings which were destined to build walls and obstacles between them. The process of building status and prestige impeded the free flow of higher educational goods between institutions – and each retreated more or less into its own silo. It was quite remarkable what was accomplished in the absence of these barriers. Critical theory helped sculpt the structures of the institutional membership and helped shape the adult outreach of these schools. The impact was mostly limited, however, to an increase in accessibility to higher education; still, it was an important harbinger of the expanded role critical theory would come to play in the future.

We can see that the growing reliance on status and prestige, culminating in college and university rankings, was grounded in the symbolic frame/leadership since that reliance had a great deal to do with how these institutions perceived themselves.

Another unique fact that helped shape this golden age at EC, sprang from the strongly held beliefs ingrained within the Church of the Brethren. Among these beliefs, was a strongly held belief in the power and the politics of egalitarianism. Thus, these strongly held beliefs energized a vision of higher education within which all had a say and all were, in some real sense, equal. Striving to distinguish one's self above the crowd might even be seen as unchristian – thus, status and prestige could negatively influence the nature of an institution of higher education (IHE) with this particular cultural milieu.

It should also be remembered that this time period included the 1960s and the 1970s – two decades of what might be characterized as generating chaotic democracy. Democratic impulses showed up just about everywhere – in curricula, admissions policies, in grading, etc. – including in the governance of a school like EC. Driven by opposition to the Vietnam War there was a loosening of curricular discipline and a plethora of teach-ins, learn-ins, and pass-fail options.

The action and consequences of a more democratic governance at EC was the Community Congress (CC) petitioned for by students and approved by the Trustees in 1970. The Center for Community Education (CCE) was established under the CC in 1972. This saw the pressure from critical theory increase on the structures of the CCE. No longer was it merely accessibility that was boosted but also a plethora of other impacts – some of which were deeply rooted. In fact, the eight transformative tasks of critical theory challenged the new adult outreach across the board. Important to the development of the CCE was a new autonomy and the beginnings of a parallel higher education track that ran alongside the more traditional one. This itself significantly challenged the status quo and threatened accepted definitions of academic quality and the power configurations that supported them, including the wide power pathway that ran through the traditional faculty ranks.

But both the CC's and CCE's challenges to the reigning ideology and hegemony and politics were short-lived. By the 1980s, a coalition of administrators and full-time faculty worked to destroy the CC particularly by stripping its democratic elements from it. This coalition invested a great deal in the growing status and prestige ranking movement, a movement which allowed scant room for adult outreach programs. As we have seen throughout our tale, the attack gathered under the banner of academic quality and the CC's sins against it, especially through the CCE. *Different than* came to mean *inferior to*. The shibboleth proved very useful for this purpose – ill-defined enough to allow many to gather beneath it but well-enough defined to allow an observer to trace the pathways of power that could claim the right of ownership.

Much of the language of the attack was rhetorical; yet when stripped away the power pathways behind it were very real and were what, in the end, counted. As we have seen throughout the story of EC, one of the most significant masks shattered by the hammers of critical theory was that of academic quality. Many arguments used this vocabulary, time and time again, to hide the power and its politics that really drove the system.

The new president, Gerhard Spiegler, sought the abolition of the CC:

> Spiegler wanted to replace the CC arrangement with a non-voting discussion body in which the faculty would make proposals on academic affairs and the student senate would make proposals on campus life matters .... Spiegler felt the current Community Congress was overstepping its bounds.

To Spiegler:

> [Its] role in matters of academic and curricular policy ... does not seem to be appropriate. The responsibility for shaping the curriculum and for educational policy issues such as grading must be placed squarely with the faculty.
>
> (Williamson, 2001, pp. 290–291)

Conclusion 89

When the dust settled in 1986, the trustees had abolished the CC and while the CCE still existed in enervated form, it was firmly under the watchful eye of the provost/dean of faculty. So, power and politics under a façade of the rhetoric of academic quality thwarted the power of critical theory to reach out to adult learners. In a real sense, the success of critical theory gave rise to the reactionary forces that would go to war with it.

By 1986, this coalition invested heavily in the growing status and prestige ranking movement which allowed little room for adult outreach programs.

With the rollback of the democratic tide, adult enrollments dwindled over the 1980s and 1990s as the CCE drifted further away from its markets. By the late 1990s, only 98 adult learners were enrolled and generating revenue in EC's undergraduate degree-completion program. The program started losing money which affected the college-wide budget and drew attention from all quarters.

Middle States' Commission on Higher Education (MSCHE), EC's regional accrediting body, reaccredited the college in 1999, based in large part on the self-study of the same year and the strategic plan of 1996. As noted above, the self-study showed a keen awareness of the dire straits the college's adult outreach had beached itself upon; yet, the authors of that study, could not envision a parallel higher education track and made it very clear that any adult outreach had to be an extension of the traditional track and full-time faculty, leaving power pathways essentially unchanged and unchallenged and the tasks of critical theory unmet. These goals bumped any goals concerning adult learners; still, the 1999 self-study called for a plan to revitalize the college's adult outreach.

I became dean of the Center for Continuing Education and Distance Learning (CCEDL), the successor of the CCE, in 2000. My charge was to grow adult outreach in enrollments and gross revenues while containing costs to increase the net contributable to the college's general fund. Most discussions with the groups I met with were not overtly put in these terms but rather in terms of increased diversity. A four-month study revealed that a drastic collapse in marketing to the adult market was responsible for the low level of adult learner activity. The old pathways of power, its politics, and its learning theories were incapable of supporting growth and expansion. The revitalization of the CE plan of 2000 (CEP 2000), was written in response to the call of the 1999 self-study; however, in its response, CEP 2000 emphasized the tasks of critical theory, new pathways of power and politics and legitimacy, and new symbolic understandings of what the college could be about.

In light of the language of the 1999 self-study, it was risky to propose a CE plan which put forth these components. But perhaps not as risky as it could have been. The CCE of 1972 reflecting widespread support through democratic protocols was, shall we say, history – a part of the college's

Conclusion

history that supported critical theory's tasks as well as empowerment through various forms of autonomy. While CEP 2000 was innovative, it could hardly be criticized as a step into the abyss because it was already part of the EC story. This fact deflected or made ineffective much criticism which might, otherwise, have proved fatal to the plan. More specifically, it was possible to position the plan as not only a revitalization plan, but as a reaffirmation plan as well. If the goal of the CEP 2000 was to cruise at 30,000 feet, the 1972 CCE constituted the runway from which takeoff occurred. Remember, the groups approving CCE 1972 and its components never rescinded that specific approval which remained on the books and to which so much of CEP 2000 returned.

Structurally, the CCEDL was designed to be nimble and flexible and to move swiftly as opportunities arose. Its main governance body was the Council on Academic Management (CAM) which included members from the CCEDL faculty, student body, alumnae, and community. At no point in its fifteen years of existence did its membership exceed 15. The president and/or provost and senior vice president were members at varying times. This helped credibility. The CCEDL dean was the permanent chair.

Strategically, we moved CEP 2000 as a revitalization/reaffirmation plan quickly through the approval process. We by-passed the old power pathways; the CAM approved it; from there it went to the Academic Affairs Committee (AAC) of the Board of Trustees (BOT) and finally to the whole BOT. Each body approved the plan overwhelmingly and by April, 2000, CCEDL staff hurried to do what was necessary to begin 5-week and 8-week accelerated courses in September of 2000. These courses were based on learning modules that were detailed, outcome-based, and which assured a standardization that supported the quality control of curricula. In its encouragement of democratic elements, clearly critical theory was operationally at work here.

Essential to the approval of the plan were two elements. The president of the college lent nervous support to the plan and the provost/dean of faculty lent more skeptical support. Neither's support was 100% nor very enthusiastic, but each supported the plan just at the level necessary to make a difference. Without this level of support, the CEP 2000 plan would have failed. The second element was the internal structure of the revitalization/reaffirmation plan itself – linking structural changes to enhanced performance – the plan presented three scenarios ranging from conservative to liberal; these scenarios were in terms of net revenues to the college. It was an art to project these financials in such a way as to make them enticing enough to the approvers, yet not unduly unrealistic. The linkage between internal-structural changes and the plan's performance scenarios proved compelling to the would-be approvers.

Conclusion

The CCEDL presented CEP 2000 to the full-time faculty through its faculty assembly; it was presented for informational purposes only; we did not seek the approval of the faculty assembly.

The next self-study and MSCHE reaccreditation protocols took place in 2009; each of the nine years between CEP 2000 implementation and the 2009 self-study saw double-digit growth for the CCEDL. By almost any indicator, growth was robust: matriculated adult learners (almost 600), net revenue contribution to the college, gross revenue contribution to the college (about 10% of total college revenues), growth of staff from four to 17 and a threefold increase in locations. Most growth was generated by a quiver of undergraduate, degree-completion programs offered in accelerated formats. The reinvigoration of CE through the SCPS had taken place. Happily, the 2009 self-study was accepting of what needed to be done to achieve these goals; the self-study of 2009 no longer viewed the CCEDL as an extension of the traditional program. In its reaccreditation letter MSCHE commended the CCEDL for its emphasis on measurable student learning outcomes and its robust academic standards. It held the CCEDL up to the traditional program as a type of model. Such commendation of a CE unit is very rare among the regional accrediting agencies.

By 2014–2015, over 800 adult undergraduates were matriculated in undergraduate, degree-completion programs and over 100 adult graduate students were matriculated in graduate programs. Gross revenues topped out at approximately $7.0 m and net revenue to the college was approximately $4.0 m. In 2014 and 2015; the CCEDL was renamed the Elizabethtown College School of Continuing and Professional Studies (SCPS). The renaming more appropriately reflected SCPS autonomy and a place where different power, politics, and critical theory had a home. The name also imparted a credibility to the different ways of doing things in the SCPS.

There is little doubt that the financial success of the SCPS did quite a bit to alter the landscape on which the college's adult learning programs roamed. EC came to depend on SCPS' financial contributions to make its macro-budget work. This dampened criticism of the new SCPS. This view of the SCPS could be both a blessing and a curse.

Secondly, the speed with which the SCPS could move toward approval was a definite advantage; this, combined with the bypassing of older, more traditional, and slower routes to approval, gave additional meaning to nimbleness and flexibility.

As performance peaked, so did the support from the president, who became enthusiastic, and from the provost/dean of faculty who became less skeptical. So, support from the top strengthened. SCPS' bedrock upper level support, without which the SCPS could not have survived, let alone move forward, remained with the trustees to whom the dean as a member of senior staff had direct access to. I made up for any BOT skepticism with my own form of brashness based on confidence in CEP 2000's scenarios, especially the most liberal scenario which projected a net contribution to the college of $500K in year five. I made the argument that if the BOT gave me this type of structure in the SCPS, I would give them back $500K in five years. Whether making the argument so personal made any difference, I'm not certain. But it did seem to personalize the process which lubricated discussions of adult learning at the college.

The president during these ten years took a more moderate view of the importance of rankings based on institutional status and prestige; this carved out more space for adult learning to be tolerated. The provost/senior vice president shared the same moderate view of the rankings system. Still, the future remains hazy. A new president in 2010 gave new life to status-based and prestige-based rankings that could once again crowd out usable space for adult learner outreach. This shift was combined with a desired change in EC's Carnegie Classification to a liberal arts institution.

Conflicts between SCPS and the traditional college still exist. The most recent incidence of this type of conflict occurred over the ownership of a new MBA program. Did the business department own it or did the SCPS own it? The BOT overwhelmingly supported the SCPS as the owner of the MBA program. With the help of the provost/senior vice president, it was a serious vote of confidence in the SCPS based on the unit's understanding of the adult learner market. SCPS knew how to treat adult learners.

Such conflict can be productive and the participants in these conflicts have a duty to find the productive elements and encourage them. For SCPS, the MBA conflict made the final version of the program better to the benefit of the adult learner. Power, politics, and critical theory, coalesced at this point in time, to make this possible. For the growth of adult learning, it does matter who's at the top and how they envision the future of the college – what's most important? Rankings? Prestige? Status? Public service? The tasks and challenges of critical theory? Answers to these questions are significant for the future of the CE units that handle adult learning. An uncertain cycle of what's most important can mean a roller coaster ride for these CE units.

Both the CCE proposal of 1972 and the CEP 2000 supported the development of SCPS' own faculty. SCPS developed a hybrid faculty – a faculty whose employment status with the college was part-time, yet who performed many tasks usually associated with full-time traditional faculty. SCPS provided base compensation for facilitating a five- or eight-week course, but bundled curricular and governance tasks which, when unbundled and completed satisfactorily, SCPS compensated by separate fee. Our facilitators were our frontline people in transmitting critical theory's tasks to the adult learners in the classroom, through the learning modules they developed and revised, through the quality of the governance tasks they performed, and through the quality of the facilitation of learning. And they were the front-line people in measuring the success of that transmission. Like the full-time faculty, they were centers of power, politics, and legitimacy creating new pathways for each.

The importance of administrative staff as carriers of power, its politics, and critical theory's values to adult learners is only slightly less than that of the affiliated faculty; this is especially true of frontline staff such as academic advisors and admissions coordinators. We hired administrative staff by rubric in a way only slightly less intense than hiring faculty by rubric. You need to take into account, though, specialized functions of staff, not found among the faculty – for example, acting as liaison with other college offices; interpreting rigid standards in a more flexible way; etc. The ability to perform these functions can be picked up by using the appropriate hiring rubrics.

Administrative staff in adult learning programs must also advocate for the adult learner; this staff will also be subject to a significant amount of stress because of the high learner/employee ratios necessary to support a respectable net.

The SCPS operated from two locations going back to the early 1950s. As of 2015, six locations bring the adult learning outreach of the college to the adult learner. Four in Lancaster County, one in Harrisburg, Pennsylvania and one in York, Pennsylvania.

Many argue that with the explosive growth of online learning, physical locations are obsolete or will be soon. While online courses have grown rapidly (67% of SCPS courses are offered online), it doesn't follow that physical locations will shrivel and die. The internet allows for a spectacular outreach that cannot be captured by a physical location. Yet most of SCPS' online users remain regional to south-central Pennsylvania and these users value personal contact on a regular basis with their advisors as they undertake their academic journey. This may mean that a physical location includes more of an office type configuration where people can meet, rather than a classroom type configuration where classes are held. Remember that to the student, any location is the face of the college. Make certain that standards associated with the college are implemented and scrupulously upheld at any location. A strong symbolic frame helps with this.

Class conflict is one of the engines of history writ small or writ large; it is a major reason why things that were, are no longer, and why things that never were, are. It is why things change on a macro- and micro- level. We have been taught the negatives of class conflict and have come to expect them. Marx's pessimistic mechanism takes into account that a social class will go on to create the very class that will overthrow it.

Conclusion

So, too, on an organizational level; the first class (or the primary class) in higher education is hungry for what they do not have and they unconsciously go about creating the second class (or the secondary class) that can give them what they want – most notably money, finances, resources. The primary class will come to hate this dependence and the weakness that comes along with it. Thus, the source of hostility and anger aimed at the secondary class and its programs lies in the depths of the primary class' own psyche. The first class will quite nonchalantly shower the second class with pejoratives and negatives of all sorts never thinking for a moment that they are really criticizing themselves. Hence, language is used to imprison the secondary class. (Especially that of academic quality). All college students are kids, including the 38-year-old single mother. The kids drink beer ignoring that 42-year-old male who sips Maker's Mark quietly in the evening at home. The presence of secondary students devalues the end educational product, the degree. The secondary programs, including their academic policies, curricula, and staff, are tainted in the eyes of these primary observers. And the revenues they generate are not really tuition, which is so tightly connected to academic programs.

Do not forget that those who run and oversee adult learning programs also create or at least strengthen a class consciousness among their students. They insist that the adult learner be honored differently, be taught differently, and live by the tasks of critical theory. In a conflictual relationship with other higher education classes, this relationship at the organizational level could: *challenge ideology, contest hegemony, unmask power overcome alienation, liberate learning, reclaim reason, practice democracy and contest bureaucratic rationality.* Thus, the creation of different classes within higher education is a joint effort with a mixture of motives. The language of the conflict can be very hurtful. The boundaries defining organizational classes are set by those who share a variety of motives. The point is that behind the hurtful language of both sides roll pathways of power, its politics, and the values of critical theory that can make a difference. Viewed from the political frame, conflict will coalesce over the distribution of resources. The symbolic frame sharpens different class identities and what they mean to those who hold them.

The questions posed and answered by this study may seem skewed to adult learning program start-ups; that is a bias that is buried deep within the study itself. But to say these findings are only applicable to this life stage of adult learning programs is to cut the story too thin. And the answers given, with a little jiggling, can be applied to all stages of adult learning program life or even to higher education itself sans such programs. The eight critical theory tasks, with some adjustment, might apply to traditional programs as well.

Conclusion 95

This widely cast finding reminds us, though, that adult learning, its programs, its faculty, its staff, its students, and its philosophies and methodologies, can grow in numbers and influence, disrupting the traditional relationships among power, politics, and critical theory. Such disruption can take on any number of forms; the salient one, at hand, being the result of a complicated adult learning growth disrupting the college's desire to join the rankings race, at least for a while, to the chagrin of powerful but aging administrators and faculty. Also, adult learning disrupted other familiar power pathways that ran through the full-time faculty ranks. On the other hand, unique characteristics of EC made practicing democracy more likely – this from a matrix of egalitarian culture, the Zeitgeist of the 1960s and 1970s, and so on.

Pathways were not only disrupted but lost a good part of their instrumentality or their ability to serve the goals they were originally designed to achieve; instead, they became institutionalized serving their own goals. As institutions, concerned with goals that benefited only themselves, they became less likely to respond to changing market conditions or to even recognize the coalescing of new markets. Thus, this configuration was no longer that of an effective instrument. The glaring self-interest of the 1999 Self-study which spoke glowingly of more non-traditional students for EC, yet only within the familiar flows of power, the familiar politics, and the familiar theories of learning, is a prime example of the result of this process of institutionalization (Quigley, 2014).

Once institutionalized, these organizational components were incapable of achieving the goals they declared they were about, adding to the façade which covered the power behind it. The growing outreach of adult learning we have seen at EC disrupted and forged new pathways, new politics, and new theories of learning in order to bypass unresponsive, crippled, and institutionalized older pathways.

These newer pathways looked like the older ones so the internal structure of the SCPS unit mirrored what seemed to be familiar. They looked similar but functioned in very different ways. Faculty, for example, was still the most powerful pathway but supported by a more streamlined and nimble power configuration that supported a more limited but powerful swath of power. Lead facilitators mirrored department chairs. SCPS faculty performed many of the same tasks as traditional full-time faculty; but performance was based on a different structural and political configuration (facilitation fee plus unbundled fees for unbundled tasks).

The answers to the why and how questions are significant not only for understanding adult learning over the period but for also understanding the workings of the pathways of power of the institutions of higher education within which adult learning is embedded.

Conclusion

As stated above, a set of different but related conclusions and lessons may be reasonably reached based on the same analysis presented here; the ones I have chosen have the advantage of being grounded in the actual experience at one specific institution.

As pointed out above, critical theory and its impacts can be hard to identify. Power and politics make themselves known in a clearer way than critical theory does. This is due partially to the fact that critical theory can easily become a shadowy immaterial outlook that disguises itself readily; but, by making more effort, it can also become a powerful, overwhelming immaterial spirit that permeates and enlivens all that it touches. So, the professional academic advisor advances critical theory by being a champion for the adult learner and *contesting bureaucratic rationality* on her behalf. This can be found quite subtly in her attitudes about and in her application of academic rules and regulations. But its presence and operation can be even more powerful when it is wielded by an adept facilitator/practitioner in the classroom.

Most of the discussions you will have about the lessons in this book will not be straight exchanges about power, politics, and critical theory. You must appreciate how threatening such exchanges can be to current stakeholders. It is as if to talk directly about them, adds to their disruptive power.

Be that as it may, these discussions will raise new sets of questions that have a wide applicability to higher education in general and the promise of fruitfulness in their suggested answers.

References

Accreditation Visiting Team. (2009). *Report to the trustees, administration, faculty, staff and students of Elizabethtown College*. Middle States Commission on Higher Education. Elizabethtown, PA: Elizabethtown College Press. Available in SCPS Office.

Bolman, L. G. & Deal, T. E. (2013). *Reframing organizations: artistry, choice & leadership*. San Francisco, CA: Jossey-Bass.

Brookfield, S. D. (2005). *The power of critical theory: liberating adult learning and teaching*. San Francisco, CA: Jossey-Bass.

Center for Continuing Education and Distance Learning (CCEDL). (2000). *Continuing Education Plan—CEP*. Elizabethtown, PE: CCEDL.

Davies, N., (1998). *Europe: A history*. New York: Harper-Perennial.

Elizabethtown College Self-Study Committee. (1999). *Elizabethtown College ten year self-study for Middle States Commission on Higher Education*. Elizabethtown, PA: Elizabethtown College Press.

Engels, F. & Marx, K. (1848). *The communist manifesto*. London: Workers' Educational Association.

Johnson, S. M. (14 July 2014). *Lecture: assuming leadership*. Harvard Graduate School of Education. Harvard Institutes for Higher Education, Institute for Educational Management.

Knowles, M. S. (1970). *The modern practice of adult education: Andragogy versus pedagogy*. New York: Cambridge Books.

Merriam, S. B., Caffarella, R. F., & Baumgartner, L. M. (2007). *Learning in adulthood: a comprehensive guide*. San Francisco, CA: Jossey-Bass.

Quigley, C. (2014). *The evolution of civilizations: An Introduction to historical analysis*. New York: Ishi Press International.

Randall, L. (2015). *Dark matter and the dinosaurs: The astounding interconnectedness of the universe*. New York: HarperCollins.

Williamson, C. (2001). *Uniting work and spirit: A centennial history of Elizabethtown College*. Elizabethtown, PA: Elizabethtown College Press.

Index

academic advisor data base support specialist 75
academic advisors 75
academic quality, rhetoric of 79–83
accreditation and continuing education plan 37–47, 89
admissions coordinators 75
Adorno, T. 7
Adult External Degree Program (AEDP) 33
affiliated faculty 51–59, 92–93
associate dean 75

Baugher, A.C. 18
Bolman, L.G. 2, 13–14, 85, 86
Brookfield, S.D. 2, 4–5, 85, 86
Byerly, R.A. 18

Center for Community Education (CCE) 32–34, 35–36, 43–47, 51, 87–89
Center for Continuing Education and Distance Learning (CCEDL) 40–41, 43–47, 51, 55, 89–91
Charlotte W. Newcomb Foundation 23
Church of the Brethren 33, 87
class conflict 7, 67–71, 94
Communist Manifesto (Engels and Marx) 70
Community College Movement 19
Community Congress (CC) 32, 35–36, 87–89
Community Education (CE) program 39–41
constitutional traditions 5–6

Continuing Education Plan (CEP 2000) 43–47, 51–54, 69, 89–92
Council for Academic Management (CAM) 44–45, 51, 90
credit transfer 18, 21, 30
critical learning theory 6
critical theory: adult education and 7–9; application of 6–7, 9–11; description of 5–6; impact of 29–31; Marxism and 4–5; as tool 2, 85–87
criticality 5–6

Davies, N. 7
Deal, T.E. 2, 13–14, 85, 86
dean of enrollment services 75
dean of student services 76
director of curriculum 76
Dixon University Center 29–30
dual-class system 12–13

Elizabethtown College (EC): accreditation and continuing education plan of 37–47; beginnings of 27–36; class conflict and 67–71; conclusions regarding 85–96; description of 1–2; faculty of 49–59, 92–93, 95; governance of 18–19, 32–34; locations for 61–65; mission of 17; rhetoric of academic quality and 79–83; second class categorization at 12–13; staff of 73–78, 93; strategic plan for 20–21, 39–40; timeline for 15–25
Engels, F. 70
EXCEL program 33
Excellence in Innovation Award 24

F&M College 22
faculty 49–59, 92–93, 95
faculty assessment process 55–59
faculty responsibilities 21–22
frames: analytical power of 13–14; description of 2–3; leadership styles and 3–4
Frankfurt Institute of Social Research 7
Fromm, E. 7

GI Bill 15, 29
governance task group 51–54

Habermas, J. 7
Harrisburg Pennsylvania Area College Center 17, 29
High, S.D. 23
Hitler, A. 7
Hoover, J.B. 23
Horkheimer, M. 7
Human Resource Frame 3
Human Resource Leadership 4

Institute for Learning in Retirement (ILR) 19
intellectual property rights 52
is/ought gap 8–9, 10

James B. Hoover Center for Business 23

Kasworm, C. 25

leadership styles 3–4
Lehigh Valley College (LVC) 17, 29
location managers 76
locations 61–65

Marcuse, H. 7
Marx, K. 7, 70, 93
Marxophobia 4

methodology, overview of 2–4
Middle States Commission on Higher Education (MSCHE) 39–40, 89, 91
Murphy, E.R. 23

National Council for Accelerated Programs (CAP) 24
Nihon University 21
Noel Levitz Adult Learner Inventory (AIL) 23
non-credit coordinator 76

office manager 76
online learning 63–64

Political Frame 3
Political Leadership 4

Randall, L. 9–10
Records and Registration (RR) office 77
revenue and expenses, recording of 11–12, 70

School of Continuing and Professional Studies (SCPS) 25, 55–59, 63–64, 69–71, 75–78, 91–93
SCPS dean 76
second class categorization 12–13, 69–71, 94
self-studies 39–42, 43, 89, 91
Spiegler, G. 88
staff 73–78, 93
status quo, challenges to 35–36
Structural Frame 2
Structural Leadership 3
Symbolic Frame 3
Symbolic Leadership 4

transformative tasks 81, 85–86